ACTIVE LEARNING

VOLCANOES & EARTHQUAKES

DK | Penguin
Random
House

Project Art Editor Jessica Tapolcai
Designers Annabel Schick, Vicky Read
Senior Editor Satu Hämeenaho-Fox
Editors Ashwin Khurana,
Sophie Adam, Lizzie Munsey
US Editor Heather Wilcox
Editorial Assistant Elise Solberg
Managing Editor Carine Tracanelli
Managing Art Editor Anna Hall
Jacket Designer Stephanie Tan
Jacket Design Development Manager
Sophia MTT
Production Editor Gill Reid
Production Controller Poppy David
Art Director Karen Self
Publisher Andrew Macintyre
Publishing Director Jonathan Metcalf

Illustrators Jeongeun Park,
Mark Ruffle, Dan Crisp

First American Edition, 2023
Published in the United States by DK Publishing
1745 Broadway, 20th Floor, New York, NY 10019

Copyright © 2023 Dorling Kindersley Limited
DK, a Division of Penguin Random House LLC
23 24 25 26 27 10 9 8 7 6 5 4 3 2 1
001–324973–Apr/2023

A catalog record for this book
is available from the Library of Congress.
ISBN 978-0-7440-5613-6

DK books are available at special discounts when
purchased in bulk for sales promotions, premiums,
fund-raising, or educational use. For details
contact: DK Publishing Special Markets,
1745 Broadway, 20th Floor, New York, NY 10019
SpecialSales@dk.com

Printed and bound in China

For the curious
www.dk.com

THE AUTHOR AND CONSULTANT

Tom Jackson has been a science writer for 25 years.
He's experienced a couple of earthquakes but has not
seen a volcanic eruption yet—although he's come
very close. Among other things, Tom studied geology at
Bristol University, and he now writes about all things
scientific. This includes everything from the history of
ideas and Stone Age tools to the search for dark matter
and the development of sustainable technologies.

John Farndon, our consultant on this book, is the
author of more than a thousand books on such topics as
science and nature, including the best-selling *Practical
Encyclopedia of Rocks & Minerals* and the acclaimed
Atlas of Oceans: A Fascinating Hidden World. He has
also contributed to many DK books, including *Earth and
Natural Wonders*. John has been shortlisted five times
for the Royal Society Young People's Book Prize.

CONTENTS

Inside Earth

The layers inside Earth have different temperatures. The hottest layers are closer to the center. These inner layers are made of very dense materials. Closer to the surface, the layers are cooler and less dense—they float on top of the inner layers.

1 Crust
This is a layer of solid rock. It is the only part of Earth that people have seen.

2 Upper mantle
This is made of a layer of solid rock and a layer of slow-moving, semi-liquid rock.

3 Lower mantle
This part of the mantle is solid rock, which is very hot and under great pressure.

4 Outer core
This layer is made of liquid metal. It is mostly iron, with some nickel.

5 Inner core
This metal ball is mostly iron and nickel, with traces of some other elements.

Earth is surrounded by a blanket of air, which is called the atmosphere.

BUILD THE PLANET
Follow the steps below to complete this picture of the inside of our planet.

1. Start by connecting the dots in order, using a dark pen. Once complete, you will have drawn a mantle plume—a big bubble of hot rock that is rising up toward the surface.

2. Next, color in the different layers. You can copy the colors from the section that has already been filled in.

COLOR IT!

No one has ever traveled to the **mantle**. It is only a few miles under Earth's surface, but it is too hard to reach.

LAYERED EARTH

Earth is not just a simple lump of solid rock. Its inside is very hot and made of a mixture of rocks and metals, which form several separate layers. Earth's outer layer is made of hard rock, with molten layers farther inside. Volcanoes and earthquakes occur when the crust moves around or cracks open.

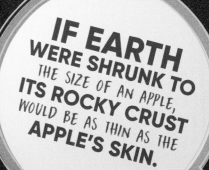

IF EARTH WERE SHRUNK TO THE SIZE OF AN APPLE, ITS ROCKY CRUST WOULD BE AS THIN AS THE APPLE'S SKIN.

WHICH IS WHICH?

Earth's crust is not the same thickness everywhere. The **oceanic crust** that forms the seafloor is much thinner than the **continental crust** under dry land. Complete the labels on this diagram to show which is which.

a ....
This crust is only about 3.7 miles (6 km) deep and is found under the sea.

b ....
This crust is 12.4–18.6 miles (20–30 km) thick but up to 31 miles (50 km) under mountains.

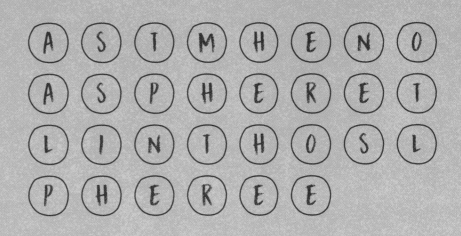

Earth's rocky crust floats on top of this molten layer, the asthenosphere, which is part of the upper mantle.

FIND THE WORD

The upper mantle has two layers of its own. The top layer, the lithosphere, is hard rock. About 124 miles (200 km) down, hotter rocks start to move—this is the asthenosphere. Cross out the letters of LITHOSPHERE and ASTHENOSPHERE. Which six-letter word is left behind?

_ _ _ _ _ _

A S T M H E N O
A S P H E R E T
L I N T H O S L
P H E R E E

FIND AND MATCH

Can you match these plate outlines with their location on the map? The name of each plate might give you a clue about where to look. Write their names on the map.

NORTH AMERICAN PLATE

PHILIPPINE SEA PLATE

COCOS PLATE

NAZCA PLATE

CARIBBEAN PLATE

ARABIAN PLATE

OKHOTSK PLATE

JIGSAW EARTH

Earth's surface is made of solid rock, with cracks running through it to make dozens of chunks, called tectonic plates. All these plates fit together like a giant jigsaw. Most of the world's volcanic eruptions and earthquakes happen where the plates meet.

MATCH IT!

a ....

b ....

c ....

d ....

e ....

f ....

g ....

h ....

Meeting plates

There are three types of boundaries between plates, as seen on the map. This depends on how the plates move in relation to each other. Dotted lines show where the boundary type is unclear.

Transform
The two plates move from side to side.

Convergent
One plate sinks down under the other.

Divergent
Plates move apart as magma rises between them.

EURASIAN PLATE

SCOTIA PLATE

AFRICAN PLATE

PACIFIC PLATE

AUSTRALIAN PLATE

INDIAN PLATE

ANTARCTIC PLATE

SOUTH AMERICAN PLATE

i ....

k ....

j ....

l ....

m ....

n ....

o ....

WHERE ARE YOU?

Can you find which tectonic plate you are on? Write it below. Then mark your home on the map to see how far from the edge of the plate you live.

....

EARTHQUAKES

Earthquakes happen when a burst of energy is released inside Earth, sending a wave of energy through the rock. When this reaches the surface, the ground shakes—it's a quake! Most earthquakes happen on or near the cracks where Earth's tectonic plates meet, known as faults.

EVERY YEAR THERE ARE ABOUT **20,000 EARTHQUAKES.**

Faults

Tectonic plates move very slowly against each other. Earthquakes occur when plates get stuck against each other for tens to thousands of years, as pressure builds and is suddenly released.

Plate
A large chunk of Earth's crust.

Fault
The place where plates meet.

Inside an earthquake

The point where an earthquake begins is called the focus. Above it, on Earth's surface, is the epicenter. Seismic waves spread out from the epicenter, shaking the ground as they go.

FOCUS

Epicenter
The point on the surface above the focus.

Seismic waves
The shaking caused by the earthquake.

SHAKE IT UP

All the shaking has jumbled up the words on these slabs of rock. Can you reorder the letters and then write the words below? There are a few clues on the picture above to help you out.

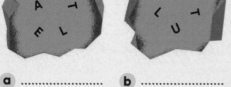

a .... b .... c .... d ....

8

WHERE IS SAFE?

Some earthquakes are bigger than others. Use the key to help you draw a circle of the correct size around each epicenter (colored dot) in the grid below. Then, can you find the one square that won't be hit by shock waves?

Coloring key

DRAW IT!

SEISMIC WAVES
FROM SOME BIG
EARTHQUAKES
CAN TRAVEL ALL THE WAY
AROUND THE
WORLD!

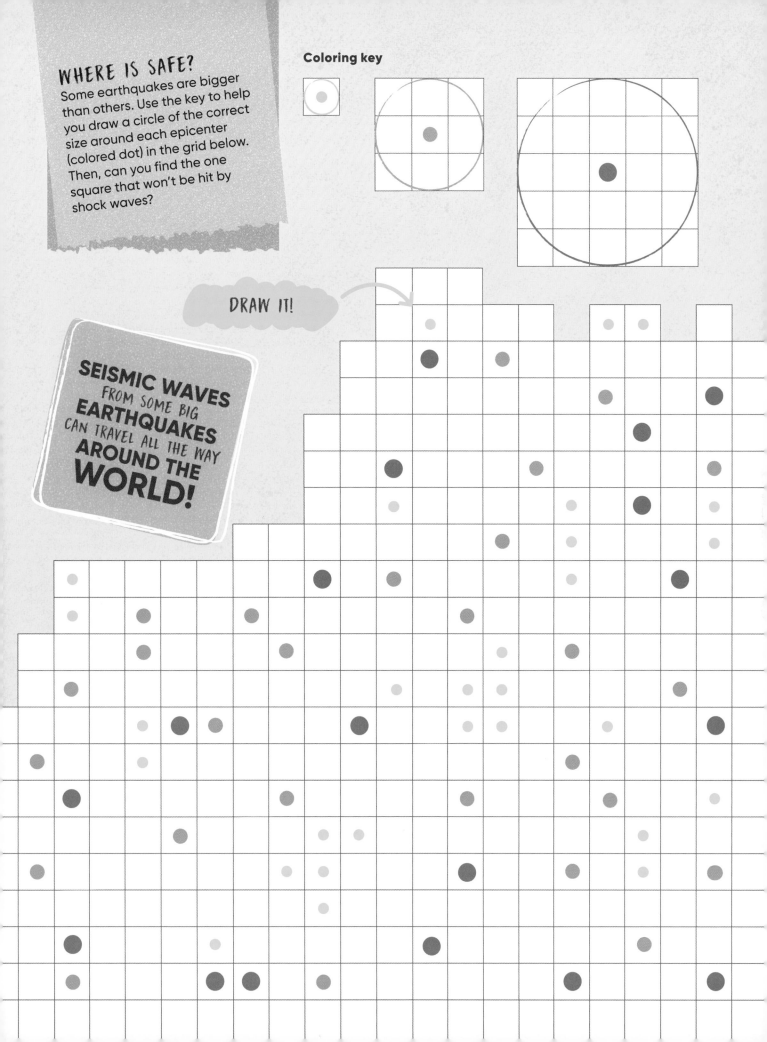

MEASURING EARTHQUAKES

How big is an earthquake? To find out, scientists use machines that monitor how much the ground is shaking. Each earthquake is given a number on the magnitude scale, which allows us to compare their sizes.

SEISMOMETERS WERE USED BY **ASTRONAUTS** TO RECORD **MOONQUAKES**— TREMORS UNDER THE SURFACE OF THE MOON.

Seismograph

A seismograph records the vibrations that occur during an earthquake. The type shown here converts the shaking of the ground into a line drawn in pen on a piece of graph paper. Modern seismometers record and display the information digitally.

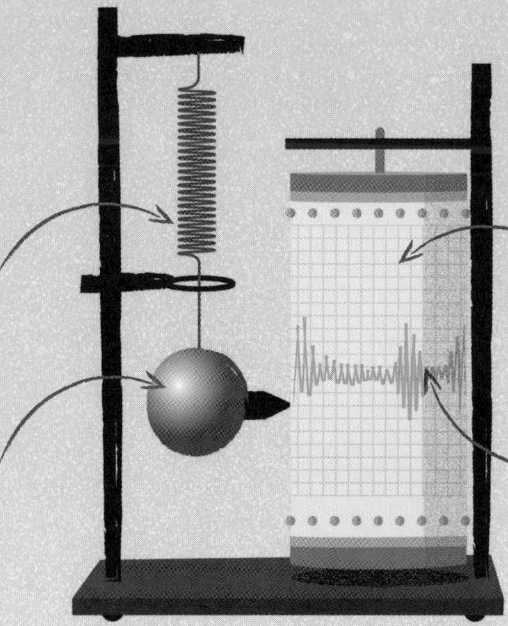

Spring
As the ground shakes, the spring absorbs the bouncing, keeping the weight still.

Weight
The heavy weight stays still, while the rest of the apparatus moves around it.

Paper
The roll of paper turns constantly, so that the pen draws a line along it.

Seismogram
The line made as paper shakes under the pen is called a seismogram.

MEASURE THE QUAKE

Scientists use seismograms to measure how powerful earthquakes are. Join the dots to complete this one. Can you see when the earthquake started?

DRAW IT!

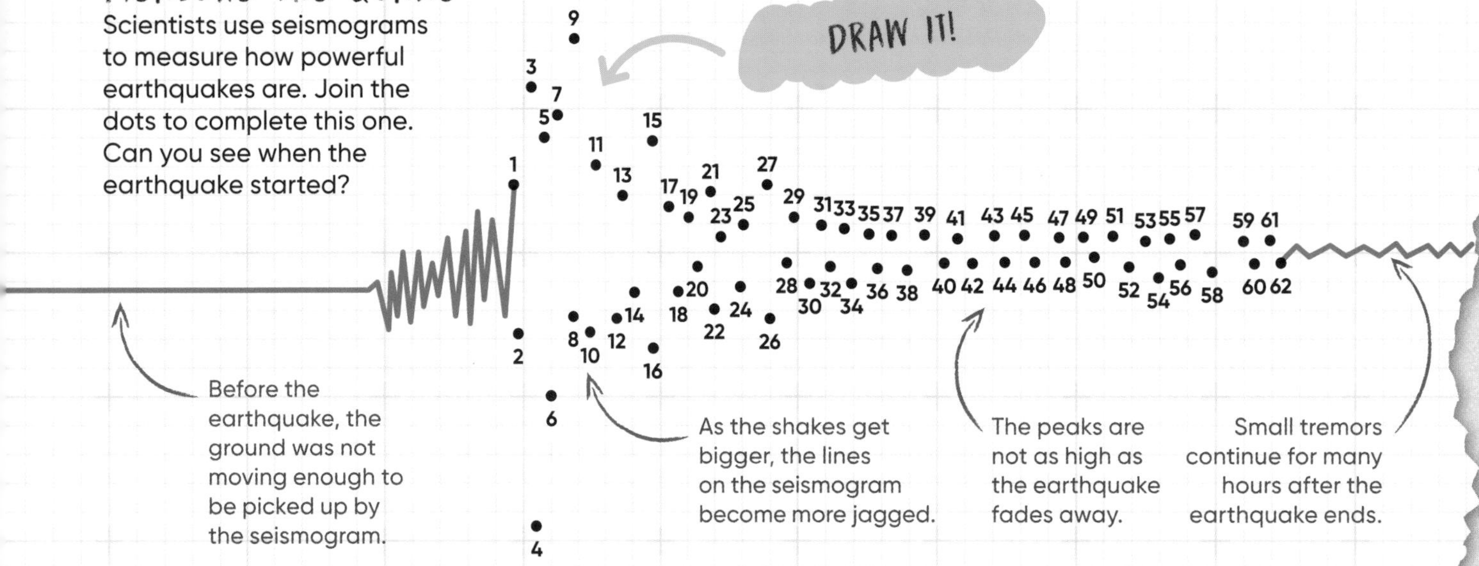

Before the earthquake, the ground was not moving enough to be picked up by the seismogram.

As the shakes get bigger, the lines on the seismogram become more jagged.

The peaks are not as high as the earthquake fades away.

Small tremors continue for many hours after the earthquake ends.

SORT THE EARTHQUAKES

The size of earthquakes is measured on the Moment Magnitude Scale (MMS). Each earthquake is given a number—the bigger the number, the more powerful the earthquake. Sort the quakes below into size order, then color the circles using the key.

COLOR IT!

5.8 Virginia, US, 2011
Shaking felt as far away as Washington, DC

4.7 Dudley, UK, 2002
Small earthquake that broke windows

6.6 Qinghai, China, 2022
Quake in the mountains of southern China

9.1 Sumatra, Indonesia, 2004
Huge earthquake that caused a colossal tsunami

7.0 Haiti, 2010
Big earthquake that knocked down buildings

DRAW THE DAMAGE

The stronger an earthquake, the more damage it can cause. The strength of shaking is measured on the Mercalli Scale. Draw pictures in the empty squares to match the descriptions.

DRAW IT!

THE LARGEST EARTHQUAKE EVER RECORDED WAS IN 1960 **IN CHILE.** IT HAD A MAGNITUDE **OF 9.5.**

Level 1
Micro-earthquake: the shaking is so slight that people don't feel it, and there is no damage.

Level 2
Some people may feel a slight shaking, but it is not strong enough to move objects.

Level 3
Objects that are not fixed, such as a hanging room light, swing around. Most people feel some shaking.

Level 4
Items stacked on shelves or in cupboards start to move, making obvious clattering noises.

Level 5
Windows break, books fall off shelves, and furniture moves around inside buildings.

Level 6
People find it hard to stay upright. The walls of buildings may begin to crack.

Level 7
Older buildings may fall down and newer buildings move on their foundations. Roads and bridges may crack.

Level 8
Most buildings collapse. Bridges, roads, and railway lines may be badly damaged.

Level 9
There is serious destruction of the affected area and widespread loss of life.

P WAVES TRAVEL THROUGH **HARD ROCK AT 3.1 MILES (5 KM) A SECOND.**

SEISMIC WAVES

Earthquakes create shockwaves that shiver through the planet. Known as seismic waves, they spread out in all directions—traveling to the surface and through Earth. Despite the damage they can cause, seismic waves help scientists learn more about Earth's hidden layers.

To the core and beyond

Body waves caused by a large earthquake can be detected far away from the focus. This is because body waves can travel through some—or all—of Earth's inner layers. The study of these waves has helped scientists prove that Earth's core is liquid.

As P waves travel between solid and liquid layers, the waves refract (bend).

FOCUS

FOCUS

P waves (primary waves)
P waves can move through solids and liquids. They pass through each layer of Earth and can be detected on the other side of the planet.

S waves (secondary waves)
S waves can only move through solids. They cannot travel through Earth's liquid outer core and are absorbed or reflected away.

Body waves

These underground seismic waves begin at the earthquake's focus and ripple up to the surface. There are two kinds: P waves (primary waves) and S waves (secondary waves).

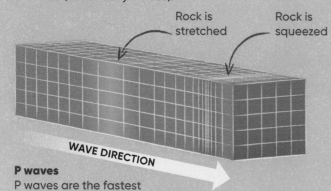

Rock is stretched

Rock is squeezed

Undisturbed rock before the wave hits

Rock moves at right angles to direction of wave

WAVE DIRECTION

WAVE DIRECTION

P waves
P waves are the fastest seismic wave and the first to appear. They move by squeezing and stretching rock underground.

S waves
S waves arrive after P waves, moving rock inside Earth from side to side and up and down.

FINISH THE PICTURE

Follow the steps below to complete this picture of what happens inside Earth during a large earthquake.

1. Using the coloring key, color in the different layers found inside Earth.

2. Starting at the focus, draw the movement of P waves and S waves through Earth's layers.

Coloring key
- Crust
- Upper mantle
- Lower mantle
- Outer core
- Inner core
- P waves
- S waves

FOCUS

COMPLETE IT!

TRUE OR FALSE?

Using what you have learned about seismic waves, read the statements below and decide whether they are true or false.

a S waves can travel through Earth's liquid core.

☐ True ☐ False

b Rayleigh waves move like ocean waves on Earth's surface.

☐ True ☐ False

c P waves stretch and squeeze rock deep underground.

☐ True ☐ False

d Love waves are the fastest type of seismic wave.

☐ True ☐ False

CHECK IT!

Surface waves

Caused by body waves arriving at the surface, these seismic waves cause the most damage during an earthquake.

The surface moves perpendicular to the wave's direction.

Rayleigh waves move in a circular motion, causing a ripple effect.

WAVE DIRECTION

WAVE DIRECTION

Love waves
Typically faster than Rayleigh waves, Love waves move Earth's surface from side to side.

Rayleigh waves
The slowest kind of seismic wave, Rayleigh waves roll on Earth's surface like ocean waves.

BUILDING FOR EARTHQUAKES

Many big cities are in earthquake zones, and some of these cities have been damaged by earthquakes in the past. Building skyscrapers in these areas comes at a risk, although proper construction techniques can minimize damage when tremors shake the ground.

Skyscraper safety

The safest buildings are low rise. Tall skyscrapers in earthquake zones have to include at least one of these safety systems to avoid serious damage.

a **Shock absorber**
A huge pendulum ball swings in the opposite direction of the shaking, balancing the building.

b **Flexible foundation**
The base of the building is on rubber bumpers, so only small shakes travel up to the main building.

c **Steel frame**
Long tubes made from flexible steel help the building bend rather than break.

d **Pyramid shape**
A pyramid is the strongest and most stable shape, as most of the weight is close the ground.

MATCH THE SAFETY SYSTEMS

Read about systems that help buildings survive earthquakes in the yellow box on the right. Then, read the clues below and match these buildings with the correct safety system.

The steel in the world's tallest building protects it when the ground shakes.

This pointed building is ready for the next earthquake.

This skyscraper's pendulum keeps it steady during earthquakes.

This huge domed arena will only feel small shakes during an earthquake.

BURJ KHALIFA, DUBAI, UAE

TRANSAMERICA PYRAMID, US

TAIPEI 101, TAIWAN

PHILIPPINE ARENA, PHILIPPINES

....

WRITE IT!

......

FIND THE CITY

This capital city has suffered earthquakes in the past and will again in future. Cross out the letters in "earthquake" to find the name of this major city. (Clue: it's in Japan.)

E T A O Q K A E O
H T U U R T K Y

_ _ _ _ _

BE AN ARCHITECT

Draw your own skyscraper on this grid. Use the instructions below to make sure it will be safe during an earthquake.

1. Draw a flexible foundation for the building below ground. This way, only small shakes will reach the main building.

2. Give your building a triangular shape and make it 50 floors tall. A pyramid is the strongest shape a building can have.

3. Draw side sections made from steel frames. These make the building more flexible.

4. Draw a pendulum ball hanging between the 30th and 40th floors. This will keep the building balanced.

5. Now, decorate it as you please! What color will it be? Are there any trees on the ground or birds in the sky?

DRAW IT!

THE TRANSAMERICA **PYRAMID** IS DESIGNED **TO SWAY** 12 IN (30 CM) FROM **SIDE TO SIDE.**

50TH FLOOR

40TH FLOOR

30TH FLOOR

20TH FLOOR

10TH FLOOR

BELOW GROUND

SHAKING UP THE LANDSCAPE

In just a few minutes, the powerful shaking from an earthquake can change the shape of the landscape completely. The quake loosens rocks, earth, and mud so they slide down hillsides. The shaking can even turn solid ground into gloopy quicksand in a process called liquefaction.

DRAW THE HOUSES

These two houses are on top of different types of soil. Read the information on liquefaction carefully and then draw each of the houses after an earthquake has shaken the ground. Which house will sink more?

Liquefaction

Soil often has water between the grains of sand and clay. During an earthquake, the shaken water pushes the grains apart, and the solid soil turns into a thick liquid. Sandy soil is most likely to liquefy.

Before an earthquake
The soil's grains form a framework, making the ground under the house firm and solid.

During shaking
The water pushes the grains apart, so the soil cannot hold anything heavy.

SANDY SOIL

CLAY/SILT SOIL

DRAW IT!

Landslides

Earthquakes often cause landslides, where the ground on a slope slides down to the bottom. There are different kinds, depending on what material falls down the mountain or hill.

Rockfall
Large rocks stuck in the soil are shaken free and roll downward, releasing more rocks as they fall.

Earthflow
During an earthquake, layers of soil and earth separate. The top layer slides down the slope.

Mudflow
Shaking liquefies the soil, so that it slides down as a thick, muddy liquid.

CHANGE THE SCENE

Landslides completely change the shape of a hillside. They can even fill lakes and block rivers! Using the color key, color in these three illustrations of the stages of a landslide to see the landscape change.

Coloring key
1. Clay/silt soil
2. Sandy soil
3. Forest
4. Grass
5. Lake
6. Sky

MUDSLIDES CAN MOVE AT SPEEDS OF UP TO 50 MPH (80 KMPH).

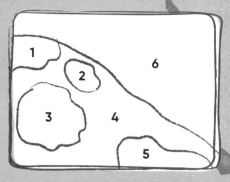

Before the landslide
The hillside is covered in trees and grass, with a lake at the bottom.

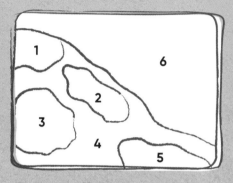

Landslide underway
The shaking releases sand and mud from near the top of the hill, which starts to move down.

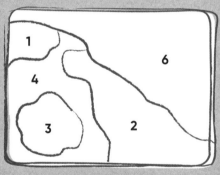

The lake is gone
The landslide has covered the slope in sand, covering some of the grass and filling the lake with soil.

FILL THE GAPS

Rearrange these letters to spell out a word linked to the effects of an earthquake. Here's a clue: this word describes big stones dropping down a slope.

O F A R R L K L C

_ _ _ _ _ _ _ _ _

TSUNAMIS

Earthquakes on the seabed make the world's largest waves, called tsunamis. A sudden shift in the seabed triggers huge ripples that spread out in all directions. The wave speeds across the ocean before crashing into the coast. A tsunami can cause waves as high as 100 ft (30 m) and flood areas far inland.

What is a tsunami?
The word *tsunami* means "harbor wave" in Japanese. The wave grows suddenly taller as it enters shallow seas near the shore.

DETECT A TSUNAMI
An early tsunami warning system, far out in the ocean, tells people on land that a wave is coming. Read the descriptions of the equipment and then write the correct name for each of the items on the empty lines.

> **Satellite**   **Surface buoy**
>   **Tsunameter**

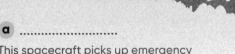

a ....

This spacecraft picks up emergency signals from surface buoys all over the world. It then alerts people on land.

The tsunami barely affects the surface when it's far out at sea.

WHEN IT IS FAR OUT AT SEA, A TSUNAMI CAN **TRAVEL AT 500 MPH (800 KMPH).** THAT'S AS FAST AS **A JET PLANE!**

b ....
This forms the link between the two other devices. It is anchored to the seabed so it does not float away.

.... **c**
This detector picks up shakes in the seabed. It sends a signal to the surface.

ANCHOR

TAKE A TSUNAMI QUIZ

Use what you have learned about tsunamis to take this quiz. Check the correct answer.

ANSWER IT!

Tsunami
The wave is only visible close to the shore, by which time it could be too late to outrun on foot.

a Each year, there are normally two tsunamis in the world. What is a tsunami caused by?

- ☐ An earthquake
- ☐ A boat
- ☐ A storm

b What does the word *tsunami* mean in Japanese?

- ☐ Tidal wave
- ☐ Harbor wave
- ☐ Earthquake flood

c In shallow water, the tsunami runs out of space and slows down. What happens next?

- ☐ It disappears.
- ☐ It rises up.
- ☐ It turns to ice.

d A tsunameter checks the seabed for quakes. How does it send out a warning signal?

- ☐ By email
- ☐ It signals to a buoy.
- ☐ It uses a loud siren.

BONUS QUESTION

How fast can a tsunami move over deep water far out to sea?

....

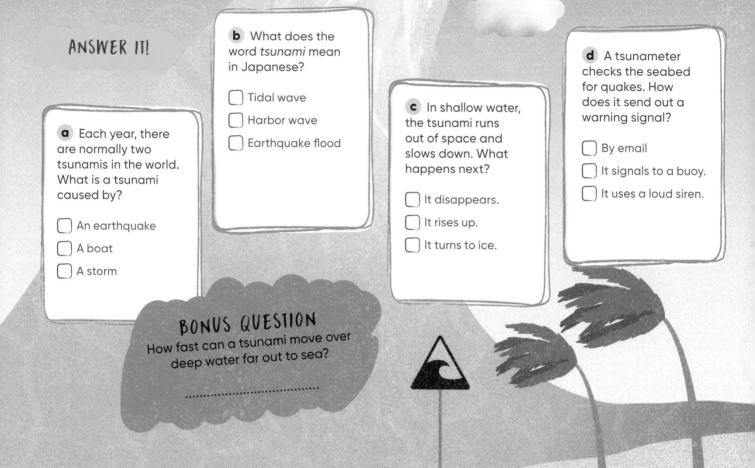

WHICH IS WHICH?

Look at these illustrations of the stages of a tsunami and then read the text below. Draw a line to match each scene with the correct description.

MATCH IT!

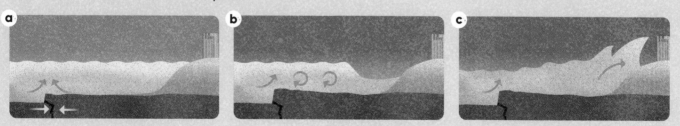

a   **b**   **c**

Making waves
The wave moves underwater at great speed. Seawater is sucked back from the shore.

Danger!
The waves grow in size as the sea becomes shallower toward the shore. A huge wave rises up.

Undersea quake
An earthquake rocks the ocean floor. This pushes up lots of water, which starts to move.

EARTHQUAKE QUIZ

Now, it's time to test your earthquake knowledge with this quiz. If you need to, go back to earlier pages to look for clues and check up on facts. Good luck!

1 What is the name for a wave that causes shaking after an earthquake?

- **a** Seismic
- **b** Electromagnetic
- **c** Sound
- **d** Tidal

2 A seismograph records the vibrations that occur during an earthquake. Modern measuring instruments record and display the information digitally.

☐ True   ☐ False

3 Earthquakes happen where the rocks underground are cracked. What is this kind of deep crack called?

- **a** Fault
- **b** Fold
- **c** Gap
- **d** Scrunch

4 Most earthquakes start underground. The epicenter is the place on the surface directly above the earthquake.

☐ True   ☐ False

5 A magnitude 5 earthquake hits your town. Which thing will NOT be happening around you?

- **a** Lights swinging
- **b** Items on shelves falling
- **c** Furniture moving inside building
- **d** Railway lines badly damged

6 Earthquakes send out P waves and S waves through the rocks. Which waves travel fastest and are felt first on Earth's surface?

....

7 Several cities are in earthquake zones. Many big new buildings have special designs that keep them standing during earthquakes. Can you identify these buildings?

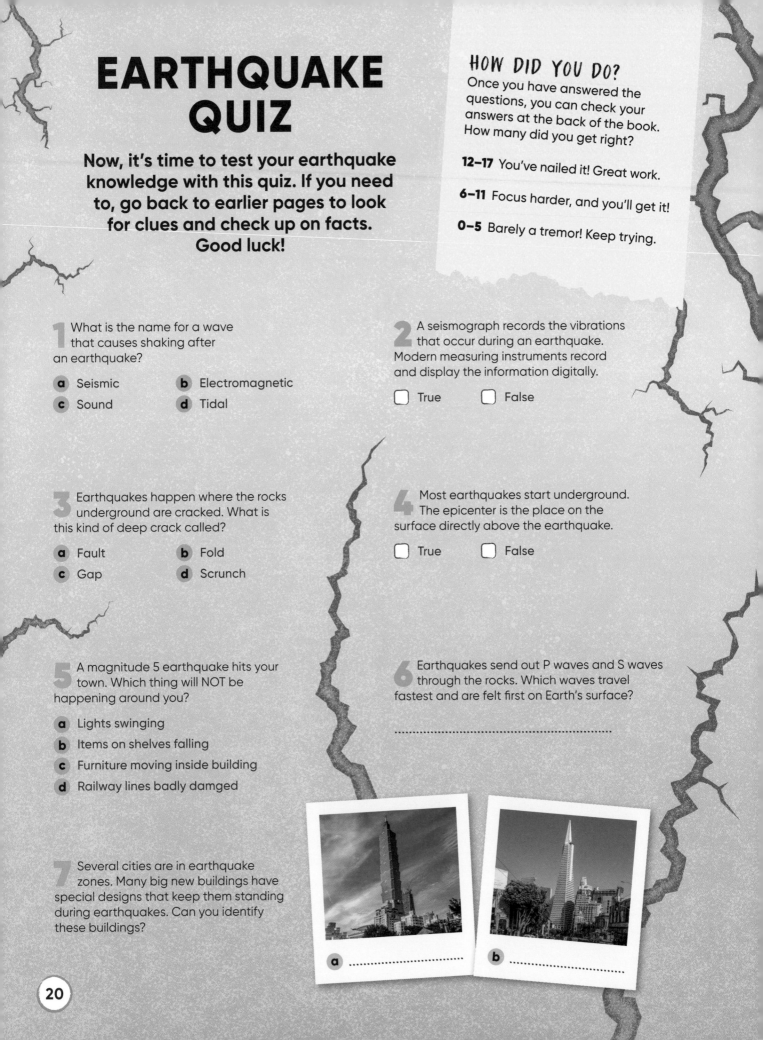

a ....   **b** ....

8 A tsunami is a big wave caused by an earthquake on the seabed. The wave rises up higher as it gets closer to the shore.

☐ True ☐ False

9 Earth's surface is made up of plates that fit together. There are three types of boundaries between these plates. Which one is NOT a boundary type?

a Convergent **b** Significant
c Divergent **d** Transform

10 In rare cases, earthquake shakes turn soil into a thick liquid that makes buildings sink. What is this called?

a Mud slumping **b** Waterization
c Liquefaction **d** Sinkation

11 The outer layer of Earth, known as the lithosphere, is made of solid rock. This rock is broken up into many separate sections called plates.

☐ True ☐ False

12 The way in which waves from earthquakes travel through Earth shows scientists that the planet has many layers inside. Can you label the two shown here?

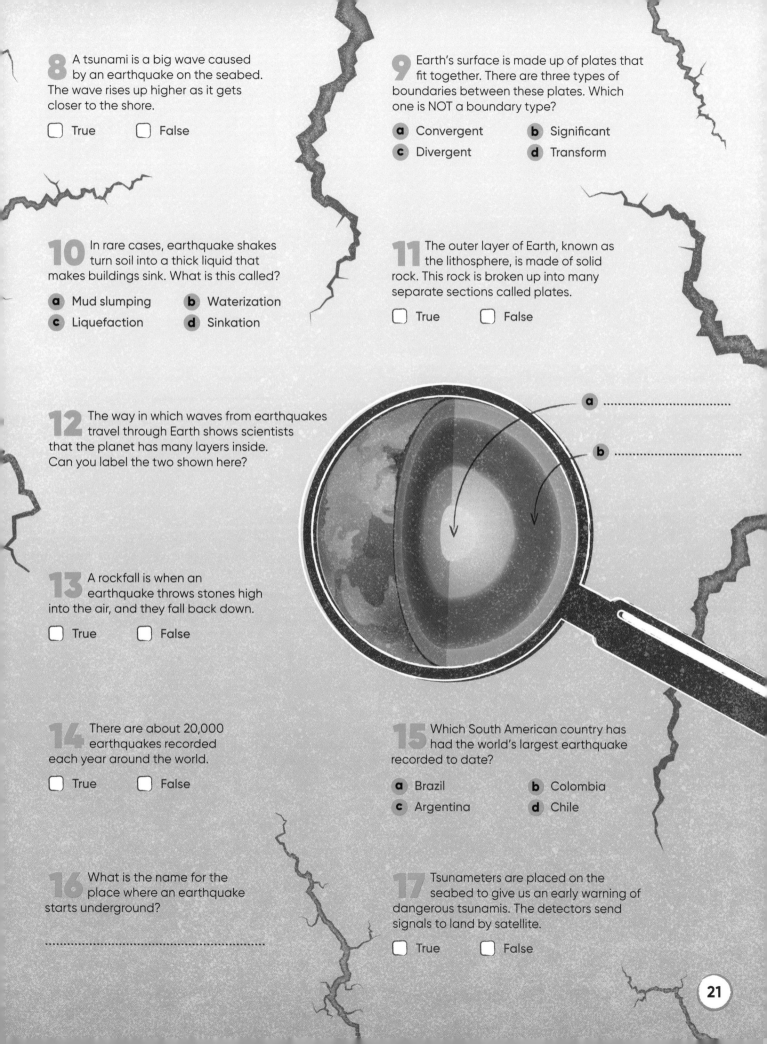

a ....

b ....

13 A rockfall is when an earthquake throws stones high into the air, and they fall back down.

☐ True ☐ False

14 There are about 20,000 earthquakes recorded each year around the world.

☐ True ☐ False

15 Which South American country has had the world's largest earthquake recorded to date?

a Brazil **b** Colombia
c Argentina **d** Chile

16 What is the name for the place where an earthquake starts underground?

....

17 Tsunameters are placed on the seabed to give us an early warning of dangerous tsunamis. The detectors send signals to land by satellite.

☐ True ☐ False

HOW VOLCANOES FORM

Volcanoes form when magma (hot, molten rock) erupts out of a crack in Earth's rocky crust. The cracks can be caused by tectonic plates moving against or away from each other. Magma from deep down in the mantle pushes up out of the cracks. Sometimes it gets stuck, and pressure builds until the volcano explodes.

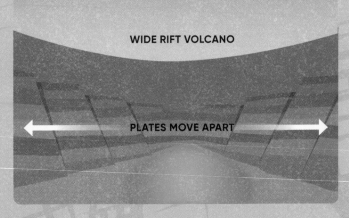

WIDE RIFT VOLCANO

PLATES MOVE APART

Rift volcano
When the plates pull apart, the pressure that keeps hot mantle rock solid is relaxed. The magma gradually wells up through the gap as the plates pull apart, which is why these volcanoes are rarely explosive.

WHICH IS WHICH?
Using the diagrams above to help you, draw lines to match each picture with the correct description.

MATCH IT!

a Kamchatka Peninsula

b Thingvellir National Park

c Kilauea volcano

Rift
This remote area of Iceland is dominated by a central volcano near a lake basin.

Hotspot
In Hawaii, this active volcano is known for its truly spectacular eruptions.

Subduction zone
Located in eastern Russia, this region has many active volcanoes close to a river (which also has hot springs).

FIND THE WORD
In these puzzles, cross out the letters to reveal two words that relate to a volcano. (Hint: cross the letters out in order.)

1. Cross out the letters in "deep" to find the name of a dark volcanic rock that rises from the mantle.

(D) (B) (E) (A) (S)
(E) (A) (L) (P) (T)

_ _ _ _ _ _

2. Cross out the letters in "subduction" to find the name of a tall thing made by subduction volcanoes.

(S) (U) (M) (O) (B) (U)
(D) (N) (U) (T) (C) (A)
(T) (I) (O) (N) (I) (N)

_ _ _ _ _ _ _ _ _

TALL STRATOVOLCANO

SINKING PLATE

ISLAND CHAIN

CRUST

Subduction zone volcano

A subduction zone occurs where one plate is pushed under another. As the sinking plate goes down, it lets water into the mantle, which melts to create magma. This rises upward and forms a volcano.

Hotspot volcano

A hotspot is a point above a continually rising plume of hot rock that moves upward from deep within the mantle. Magma forms as the rising mantle melts. The magma forces a path through Earth's crust to form a volcano.

FINISH THE PICTURE

Determine which kind of volcano this is by looking at the types above and then draw what is happening deep underground. Don't forget to draw any plate activity!

DRAW IT!

BONUS QUESTION

Which type of volcano is being formed here?

....

INSIDE A VOLCANO

There's much more to a volcano than its rocky outside. Volcanoes are openings in Earth's surface, where liquid rock bubbles up from inside the planet and escapes through channels called conduits and vents.

THERE ARE ABOUT
20 VOLCANIC
ERUPTIONS
HAPPENING AROUND
THE WORLD
AT ANY POINT IN TIME.

MATCH IT!

WHICH IS WHICH?
Draw lines to match each picture below to the correct description. You can use the diagram below to help.

a

Magma chamber
The heart of the volcano—a pool of superhot, molten rock

b

Lava flow
A slow-moving trickle of lava that spills down the side of a volcano

c

Secondary conduit
A magma pipe that branches off from the volcano's main conduit

d

Secondary vent
An opening on the volcano's side, smaller than the main vent

e

Volcanic ash
Tiny bits of magma that explode out of a volcano and cool in the air

Ash cloud

Lava bombs

Secondary vent

Secondary conduit

Magma chamber

Main vent

Main conduit

Lava flow

Layers of hardened lava and ash

Volcano anatomy

Volcanoes occur where magma (liquid rock) rises up from inside Earth. Magma builds up in a chamber, deep underground. During an eruption, it travels up the volcano's conduits and bursts out of vents as lava or ash. Each eruption adds another layer of cooled and hardened lava to the outside of the volcano.

BUILD THE VOLCANO

Follow these instructions to complete this volcano diagram. For the best results, work through the numbered steps in order:

1. Draw secondary conduits branching off the volcano's main conduit. They should end along the sides of the volcano.

2. Add some lava exploding out of the main vent and dribbling out of your new secondary vents.

3. Continue the pattern of layers of hardened lava and ash on the left side, then draw and color the layers on the right side.

4. Add dark ash swirling inside the volcano's ash cloud.

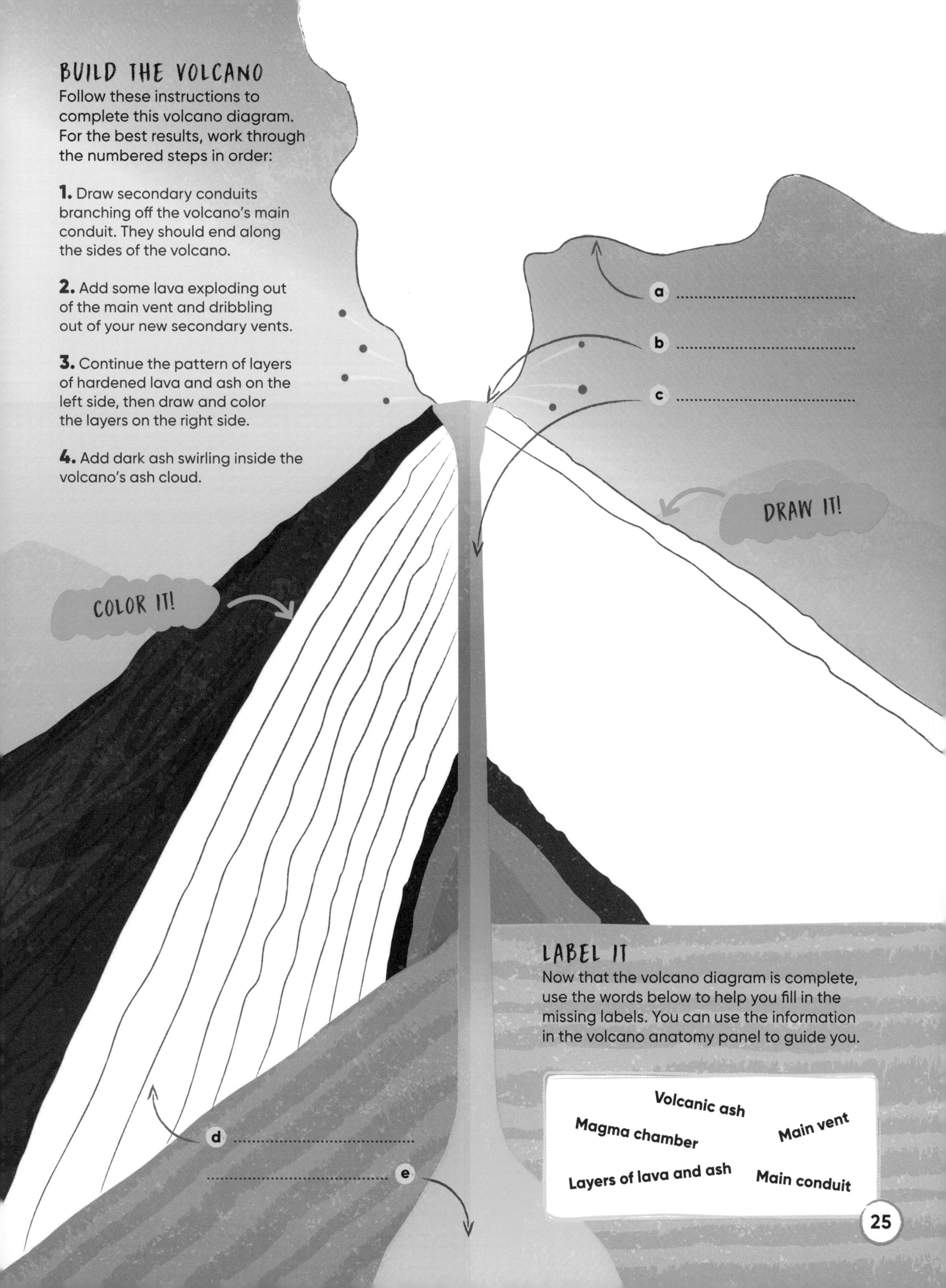

COLOR IT!

DRAW IT!

a ....

b ....

c ....

d ....

e ....

LABEL IT

Now that the volcano diagram is complete, use the words below to help you fill in the missing labels. You can use the information in the volcano anatomy panel to guide you.

Volcanic ash

Magma chamber

Main vent

Layers of lava and ash

Main conduit

25

WHICH VOLCANO?

Volcanoes can be sorted into types based on their size and shape. What a volcano ends up looking like depends on how much lava and ash come out of it during eruptions and how explosive those eruptions are.

WHICH IS WHICH?

Use what you have learned from the volcano types panel to help you tick the box showing the correct type for each of these volcanoes.

Volcano types

There are four main types of volcano. Shield volcanoes are the widest, while stratovolcanoes are the tallest and easiest to recognize.

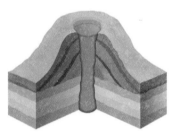

Cinder cone
A small, steep volcano formed from piles of ash and pumice flung out of the crater

Shield volcano
A big volcano with gently sloping sides, formed from many layers of runny lava

Stratovolcano
A massive, steep-sided volcano made from a mixture of ash and lava

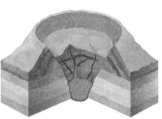

Caldera
A wide, deep crater that forms when so much magma erupts that a volcano collapses in on itself during an eruption

Whakaari,
New Zealand
☐ Stratovolcano
☐ Shield volcano

Mountain of Lagi,
Canary Islands
☐ Cinder cone
☐ Caldera

Erta Ale,
Ethiopia
☐ Stratovolcano
☐ Shield volcano

Karymsky,
Russia
☐ Shield volcano
☐ Stratovolcano

Santa Ana Volcano
crater lake, El Salvador
☐ Shield volcano
☐ Caldera

Skjaldbreiður,
Iceland
☐ Shield volcano
☐ Caldera

CHECK IT!

MAKE A VOLCANIC CHART

Complete this flow chart showing the four main types of volcanoes. You will need to use the questions on the chart to help you decide which volcano type goes where, then write the names and draw examples.

1
Does it have gently sloping sides?

No

Yes

Yes

2
Is it a large volcano?

No

No

3
Does it have a huge crater at the top?

Yes

a ....

b ....

c ....

d ....

DRAW IT!

DRAW CINDER CONES

Cinder cones are the smallest volcanoes, and they can form very fast. Sometimes, they appear in just a few days. These little volcanoes often grow on the sides of larger volcanoes. Draw a slope here with three cinder cones.

Cinder cones on Mauna Kea, Hawaii

DRAW IT!

THE RING OF FIRE

The edge of the Pacific Plate is known as the Ring of Fire, because nearly two-thirds of the world's active volcanoes are located here. It runs from the Aleutian Islands in Alaska down the coasts of North, Central, and South America and up through New Zealand, New Guinea, the Philippines, Japan, and Kamchatka (Russia). Lined up, these volcanoes would go nearly all the way around Earth!

Clashing plates

The Pacific Ocean's seabed lies on a tectonic plate that is being pushed under other plates. This process creates a string of volcanoes.

Map key
- Plate boundary
- Ring of Fire
- Volcano

NINE OUT OF 10 **EARTHQUAKES** HAPPEN AROUND **THE RING OF FIRE.**

MOUNT FUJI

LOCATION: ....

TYPE: *Stratovolcano*

HEIGHT: ....

LAST MAJOR ERUPTION: *1707*

WRITE IT!

LEARN THE FACTS

The Ring of Fire has many well-known volcanoes. Use the word box to fill in these fact cards about famous volcanoes.

MOUNT ST. HELENS

LOCATION: *Washington State*

TYPE: ....

HEIGHT: *8,363 ft (2,549 m)*

LAST MAJOR ERUPTION: ....

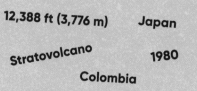

12,388 ft (3,776 m)   Japan

Stratovolcano   1980

Colombia

NEVADO DEL RUIZ

LOCATION: ....

TYPE: *Stratovolcano*

HEIGHT: *17,457 ft (5,321 m)*

LAST MAJOR ERUPTION: *2016*

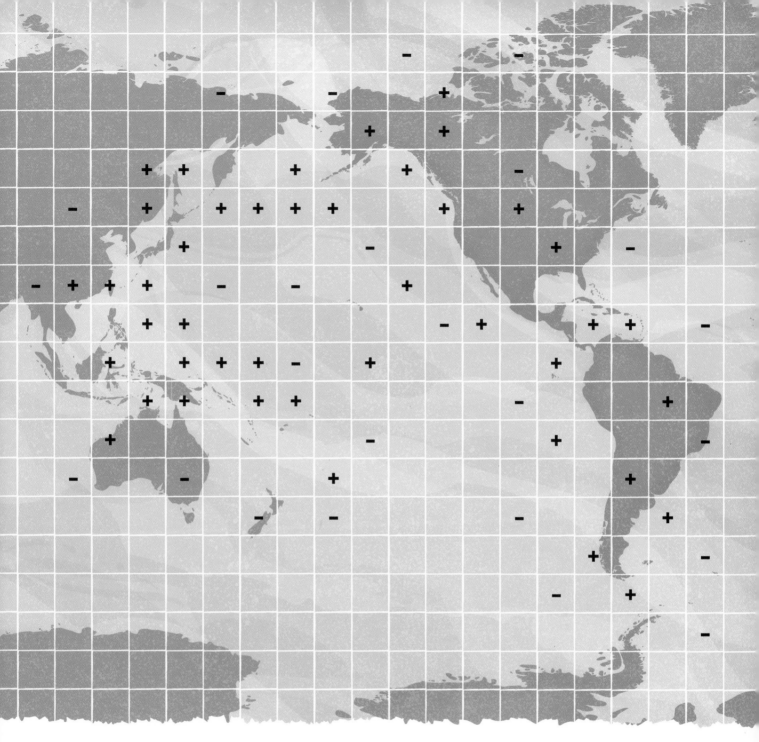

LOCATE THE VOLCANOES

Figure out where the volcanoes are hidden in the map above. They must be next to a plus sign (+) but can't be next to a minus sign (–). Here's an example to show you how it works.

1. Start by making crosses in all the squares touching a "–".

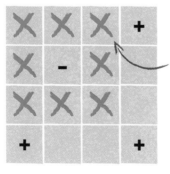

There can be no volcano in a square that is crossed out.

2. Draw volcanoes in all remaining squares that are next to a plus sign "+".

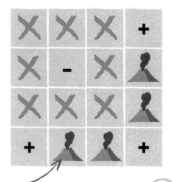

The volcanoes can't be next to a minus sign.

29

LAVA!

When hot, molten rock from deep inside Earth erupts onto the surface, it becomes lava. A stream of this red-hot liquid is called a lava flow. The speed at which lava moves depends on the texture of the lava and the slope over which it flows.

FILL IN THE FLOW CHART

Use the information in the lava-types panel to help you fill in the missing sections of this flow chart. The answers you will need are all given in the panel below.

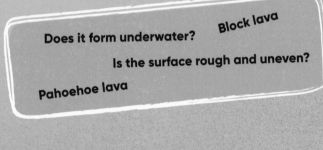

Does it form underwater? Block lava

Is the surface rough and uneven?

Pahoehoe lava

Lava types

Lava can be grouped into categories depending on how it looks, how it moves, and where it is found.

Pahoehoe lava
This kind of lava forms crusts that can have hot liquid oozing underneath them.

Block lava
This lava is thick and slow. The top cools into blocky chunks of rock.

Pillow lava
These rounded lumps form underwater. The liquid lava inside them slowly solidifies.

Aa lava
This lava rips itself apart as it flows, resulting in a rough, uneven surface.

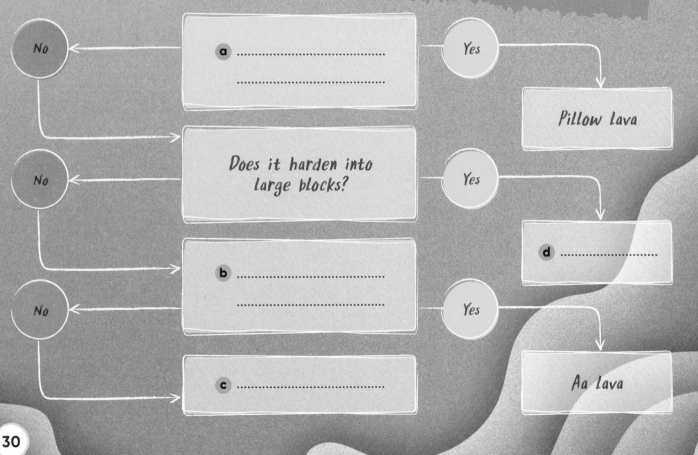

No ← a .... → Yes

Pillow lava

No ← Does it harden into large blocks? → Yes

d ....

No ← b .... → Yes

Aa lava

c ....

WHICH IS WHICH?

Lava moves in a number of different ways—it can bubble, pool, harden, or explode. Use the information in the center of the circle to fill in the missing labels for each of these pictures.

WRITE IT!

a

Pahoehoe lava is thin and runny. It cools slowly into smooth or wrinkled surfaces.

Lava lake

Into the sea

Slow and steady

Explosion

Runny river

b

Some volcano craters contain vast pools of bubbling lava.

c

During an eruption, spurts of lava are shot up into the air.

e

Some lava travels slowly, creating blobby patterns as it hardens.

d

If it flows into a body of water, lava is hot enough to turn the water into steam.

AT A VERY HOT
**2,192°F
(1,200°C),**
LAVA IS THE
HOTTEST
THING ON
EARTH'S SURFACE.

FIND THE LAVA

Which type of lava only forms underwater? Cross out the letters of the words LAVA and PAHOEHOE, then rearrange the remaining letters to spell out the answer.

(H) (I) (V) (A) (O) (W) (L) (A)

(A) (L) (H) (V) (A) (P) (A) (P)

(O) (E) (L) (O) (E) (L)

WRITE IT!

_ _ _ _ _   _ _ _ _

VOLCANIC ROCKS

The rocks that form volcanoes started as magma, lava, or ash. These are called igneous rocks. Magma that erupts onto Earth's surface as lava, or explodes as ash, forms rocks called extrusive rocks. Magma that cools and solidifies underground forms intrusive rocks.

TWO-THIRDS OF ALL THE WORLD'S ROCK WERE FORMED FROM MAGMA AND LAVA.

The rock cycle

There are three types of rocks on Earth—igneous, metamorphic, and sedimentary. All three are linked by a process called the rock cycle, which transforms rocks from one type into another over millions of years.

Igneous
These rocks form when molten rock hardens and becomes solid. This can happen above or below Earth's surface.

WEATHERING

MELTING

HEAT AND PRESSURE

MELTING

Rocks that get pushed deep underground melt back into magma.

Water, wind, and ice wear away at rocks, eventually turning them into dust and sand.

Being squeezed and heated changes a rock's structure.

Sedimentary
These rocks form when grains of other rocks are squeezed and/or cemented together.

HEAT AND PRESSURE

WEATHERING

Metamorphic
Metamorphic rocks form when older rocks are heated and squeezed, deep inside Earth.

FILL THE ROCK

As liquid rock cools, the minerals inside it form crystals. These grow and join together until they form solid igneous rock. Use colors to complete these diagrams of the crystallization process.

LIQUID ROCK

GROWING CRYSTALS

SOLID ROCK

COLOR IT!

COMPLETE THE ROCK-DOKU

Fill in this grid by drawing colorful lumps of rock. Each rock should appear only once in each row, once in each column, and once in each smaller, six-square grid. Then, answer the bonus question below.

Key

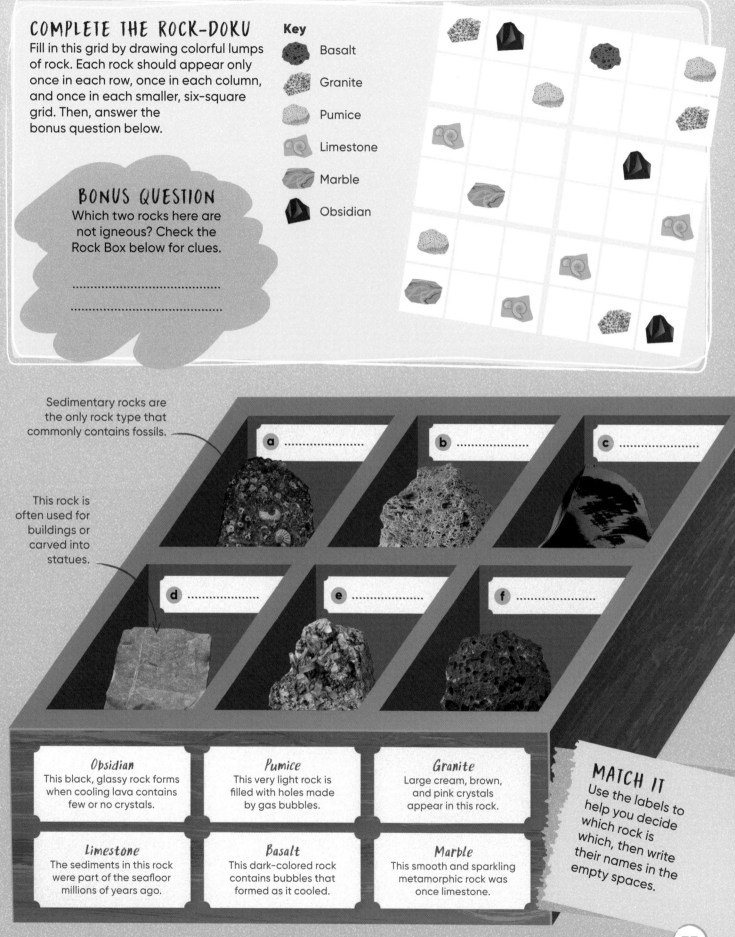

Basalt

Granite

Pumice

Limestone

Marble

Obsidian

BONUS QUESTION

Which two rocks here are not igneous? Check the Rock Box below for clues.

....

....

Sedimentary rocks are the only rock type that commonly contains fossils.

This rock is often used for buildings or carved into statues.

a ....

b ....

c ....

d ....

e ....

f ....

Obsidian
This black, glassy rock forms when cooling lava contains few or no crystals.

Pumice
This very light rock is filled with holes made by gas bubbles.

Granite
Large cream, brown, and pink crystals appear in this rock.

Limestone
The sediments in this rock were part of the seafloor millions of years ago.

Basalt
This dark-colored rock contains bubbles that formed as it cooled.

Marble
This smooth and sparkling metamorphic rock was once limestone.

MATCH IT
Use the labels to help you decide which rock is which, then write their names in the empty spaces.

LAVA CAVES

Long after a volcanic eruption has ended, explorers often find a network of caves under the site of the eruption. The caves were once channels for hot, liquid lava, but they are now filled with fascinating rock formations.

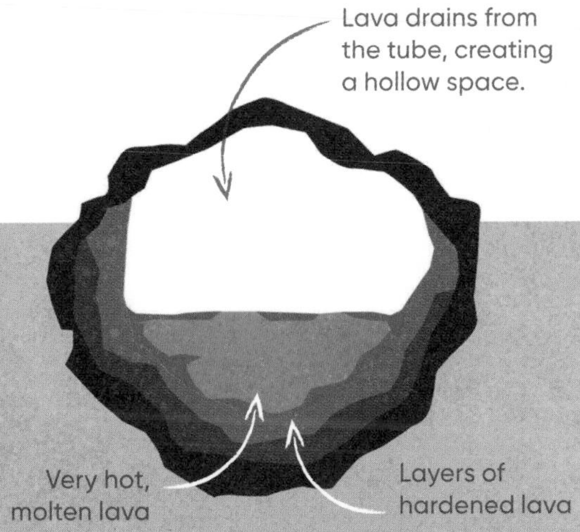

Explore inside

Lava caves contain rock features such as lavasicles and pillars, which are formed as the lava inside a lava tube drains away and cools.

How a lava tube forms

A lava tube is created when lava flows away from a volcano in a particular way. As the lava cools, it hardens around the edges, creating a circular tube of rock. Liquid lava continues flowing through the tube.

Lava drains from the tube, creating a hollow space.

Very hot, molten lava

Layers of hardened lava

MATCH THE STAGES

The descriptions below explain the stages in the creation of a lava tube. Draw a line between each description and its matching illustration.

MATCH IT!

1 Hot, molten lava begins to flow.

2 As the eruption continues, the lava flow becomes thicker.

3 The lava begins to cool, hardening around the edges.

4 Gradually, more lava hardens, forming a rocky roof.

5 Once the molten lava has drained away, a tube is left.

THE KAZUMURA **LAVA CAVE** IN HAWAII IS **40.7 MILES** (65.5 KM) LONG.

Lavasicles
These sharp spikes hang down from the roof.

Lava pillar
A lava pillar forms when a dollop of hot lava oozes all the way down to the floor.

Elephant's foot
These spiky blobs of rock are created by lava bubbling up through a hole in the floor.

COMPLETE THE FEATURES

The labels are pointing at rock features inside the lava cave—but where are they? Read the clues in the labels and use the picture on the left to help you draw in the missing features.

DRAW IT!

ERUPTIONS

During very large explosive eruptions, pumice, ash, and pieces of the volcano can be blasted high into the stratosphere. Most of the volcano falls into the emptying magma chamber, where it forms a caldera. At other times, volcanoes can erupt less dramatically, with lava slowly oozing out onto the surface.

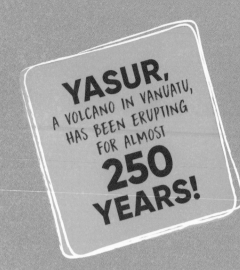

YASUR, A VOLCANO IN VANUATU, HAS BEEN ERUPTING FOR ALMOST **250 YEARS!**

FIND THE PATH

The magma in this volcano needs to find its way to the surface. Once it reaches the surface, red-hot magma is called lava. Find the route through the maze.

FINISH HERE!

Magma texture

Depending on what is in the magma and how pressurized it is just before an eruption, magma can either be thick like peanut butter or thin and runny like syrup.

Thick magma

Explosive volcanoes erupt because thick magma cannot flow out. Gas bubbles form, swell, and rip the magma apart in an explosion.

Thin magma

Volcanoes that do not erupt explosively have magma that is thinner and runnier when it reaches the surface and then flows out slowly as lava.

START HERE!

LOCATE THE ERUPTION

Massive volcanic eruptions have occurred around the world. Using the coordinates for each volcano, can you locate their position on the map below?

Coordinates key

▲ Mount Tambora (S,4) ▲ Kuwae (V,3)

▲ Kolumbo (M,7) ▲ Long Island (U,4)

▲ Huaynaputina (G,3)

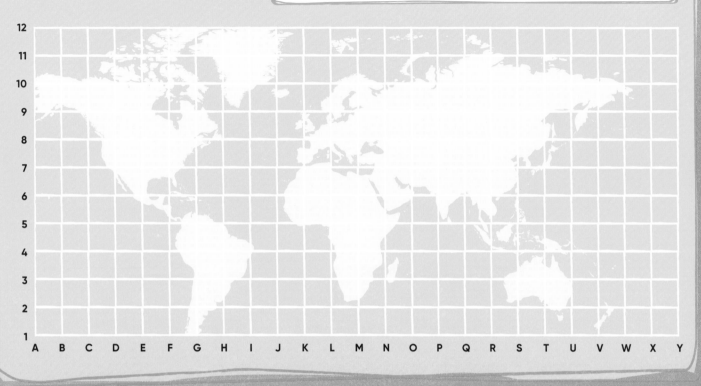

CAN YOU FEEL THE PRESSURE?

The more pressure magma is under, the more explosively it is likely to erupt. Solve the equations below and then circle the highest number. This volcano is likely to have the biggest, most explosive eruption.

a

(17 + 28)
÷ 5 =

....

b

(6 × 7)
– 25 =

....

c

(20 ÷ 4)
× 3 =

....

TYPES OF ERUPTION

When we think of a volcanic eruption, we often imagine a huge explosion with a tower of ash rising above it. Some eruptions do look like this, but not all of them—lava can bubble up slowly or burst up in fountains, and some eruptions have no ash cloud at all. Different types of eruption happen at different speeds. Some are over in minutes, while others continue for centuries!

STROMBOLI, A VOLCANO IN ITALY, HAS BEEN **ERUPTING** CONTINUOUSLY FOR AT LEAST **2,000** YEARS.

Eruption types

There are six main types of volcanic eruption. The differences between them depend on whether lava, ash, or a mixture of both is thrown out of the volcano.

Icelandic
The vent for these eruptions is a long crack in the ground. There is usually no ash cloud.

Hawaiian
This type of eruption throws fluid lava into the air as fountains that feed lava flows. There is usually no ash cloud.

Plinian
This kind of eruption happens when gas-rich magma explodes out of the vent, creating a huge ash cloud that can rise into the atmosphere.

DRAW THE ERUPTIONS

Read the hints on these cards and the information given above. Then, draw the correct type of eruption on each of the cards.

DRAW IT!

a Only lava comes out of the volcano's vent.

b This eruption can reach Earth's atmosphere.

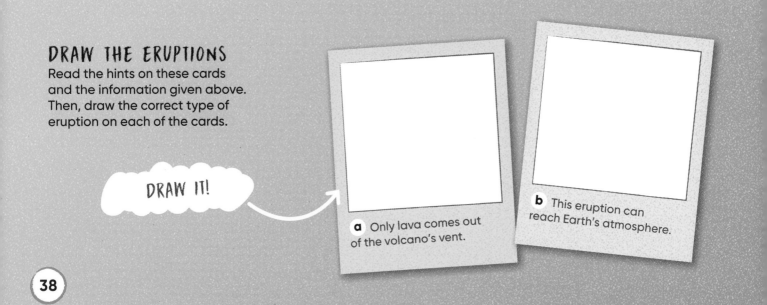

WHICH IS WHICH?

Look closely at these pictures. Can you figure out which eruption type is shown in each of them? Write the answers in the spaces below.

IDENTIFY IT!

a

b

....

c

....

d

....

e

f

....

....

....

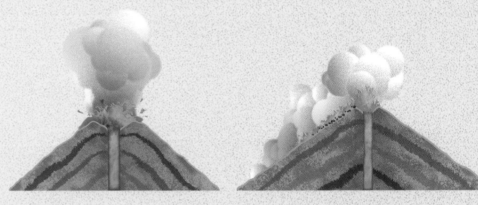

Vulcanian
This small eruption occurs when gas pressure builds inside the volcano. An explosion releases the pressure and produces a small ash cloud.

Strombolian
This type of eruption happens when large gas bubbles rise through liquid magma and explode at the surface. It can produce a series of lava fountains.

Pelean
This is when lava forms a dome that collapses, producing pyroclastic flows —currents of hot ash and gas that sweep down the side of the volcano.

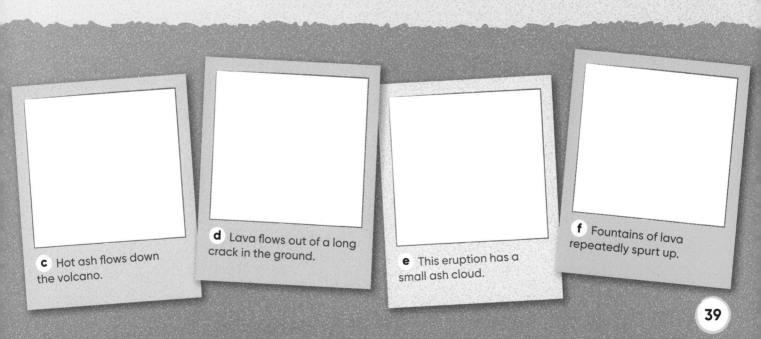

c Hot ash flows down the volcano.

d Lava flows out of a long crack in the ground.

e This eruption has a small ash cloud.

f Fountains of lava repeatedly spurt up.

PYROCLASTIC ERUPTIONS

Not all volcanoes throw lava up into the air. Even more deadly are pyroclastic flows and surges—mixtures of rock, ash, and gas that can run down a mountainside as fast as a speeding car, burning and burying everything in their path.

Sudden death
A pyroclastic surge can move very fast. It can rise over and around obstacles—even ridges hundreds of feet high—and cross water.

Flows and surges
A pyroclastic flow has two layers: the lower layer contains large rocks, ash, and hot gases, and the upper layer is a cloud of hot ash and gas. A pyroclastic surge is mostly a cloud of hot ash and gas.

Pyroclastic flow
The lower layer hugs the ground, while the ash cloud billows up into the sky, traveling far away.

Pyroclastic surge
There are no obvious layers. The cloud of gas and ash swirls around more and more as it moves downhill.

Rocks
Large rocks are being flung down the slope.

Ash cloud
A cloud of hot ash moves over the top of the rock layer.

COLOR IT!

a ....

WHICH IS WHICH?
Which of these two images shows a pyroclastic **surge**, and which shows a **flow**? Label volcanoes A and B correctly and then finish coloring the eruptions.

Burning trees
The gas is hot enough to set trees on fire.

COLOR IN THE ISLAND

In 1902, a giant volcano—Mount Pelée—in Martinique released a pyroclastic flow that covered a large area of the small Caribbean island in about three minutes. Use the key to color in the map to see how the landscape looked in 1902.

Coloring key

1 Pyroclastic flow after eruption
2 Upper mountainous region
3 Lower mountainous region
4 Forested areas

COLOR IT!

A BIG FLOW CAN COVER LAND IN ASH **656 FT** (200 M) DEEP!

Ash cloud
The cloud of ash and gases swirls as it moves downward.

FIND THE VOLCANO

In the letter jumble below, cross out the letters in the words PYROCLASTIC and ERUPTION to find the name of the volcano that erupted in Martinique in 1902. The remaining letters will spell out the answer.

b ....

```
        E
    P   A   E
  O  T E  R  P
  C   L  I  C  Y
  R   L  O  P  E
  S   T   O  U  I
```

FILL IT IN!

_ _ _ _ _

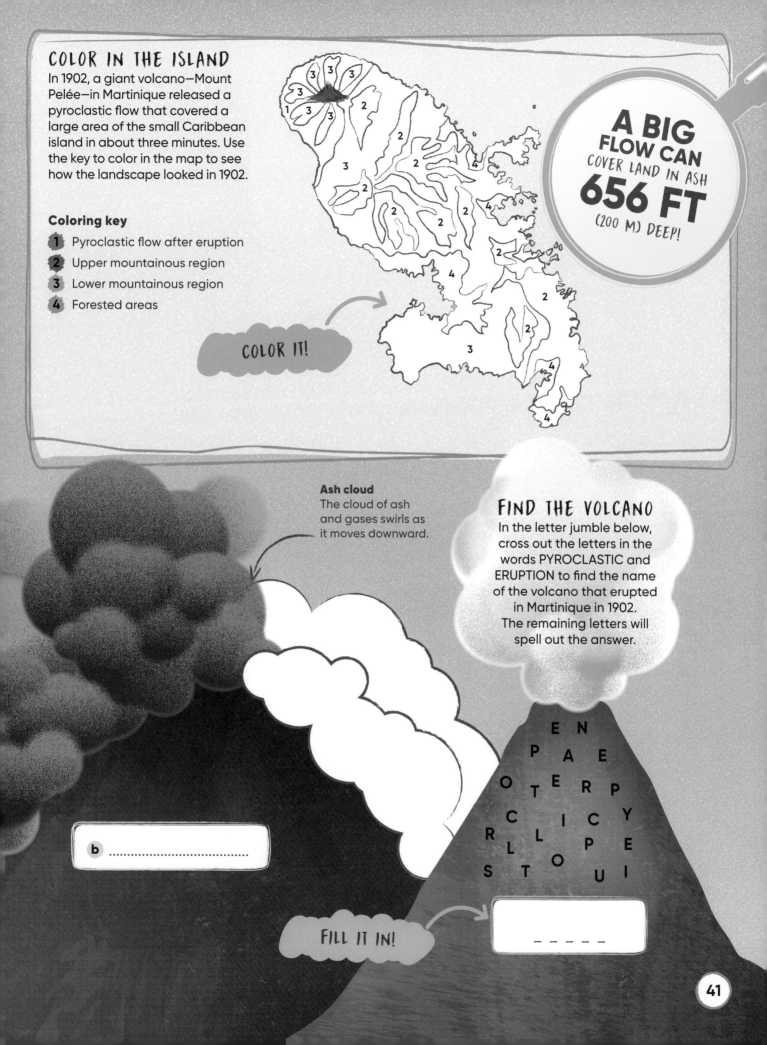

VOLCANIC FALLOUT

The power of eruptions throws vast amounts of gas, ash, and rock into the sky. What goes up must come down, and all this material will eventually fall out of the sky. Where the fallout lands depends a lot on how heavy its grains are. Sometimes, specks of volcanic ash travel right around the world!

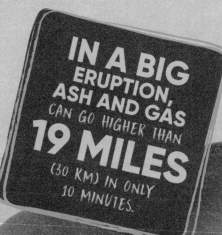

IN A BIG ERUPTION, ASH AND GÁS CAN GO HIGHER THAN **19 MILES** (30 KM) IN ONLY 10 MINUTES.

Dangerous material

A volcanic ash cloud contains poisonous—and smelly—gases, and breathing in the hot ash and gas can burn your lungs. The scientific word for the solid materials hurled from volcanoes is *tephra*. Three main kinds are shown in this illustration.

Lava bombs
These blobs of magma cool in mid-air and form solid rocks larger than 2.8 in (7 cm).

Lapilli
Shattered pieces of magma like these are 0.08–2.5 in (2–64 mm) in size.

0.6 miles (1 km)

15.5 miles (25 km)

HOW FAR WILL I GO?

These magnifying glasses give a close-up view of different types of volcanic fallout. Match each one to the distance it travels from the volcano and draw it in the empty circles.

DRAW IT!

LAPILLI

VOLCANIC ASH

LAVA BOMBS

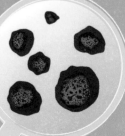

TRACK THE ERUPTION

Within three days in 2010, an eruption at Eyjafjallajökull in Iceland sent a high cloud of tiny specks of ash all over most of western Europe. To see how the cloud spread, color the yellow area first, then the red, and last the purple.

The ash cloud could damage jet engines, so all flights in the affected areas were banned for more than a week, until the ash fell back to the ground.

Coloring key

〰 April 14, 12pm

〰 April 15, 6am

〰 April 17, 6am

Volcanic ash
These are tiny specks of exploded rock that are easily blown in the wind.

620 miles+
(1,000 km+)

CRACK THE CODE

What is the word for all the solid material that is thrown from an erupting volcano? Decode this message to find out. Replace each number with a letter, where A = 1, B = 2, C = 3, and so on.

20 – 5 – 16 – 8 – 18 – 1

_ _ _ _ _ _

NAME THE FALLOUT

Using what you have learned about different kinds of volcanic fallout, label these photographs. There is one picture for each type of fallout.

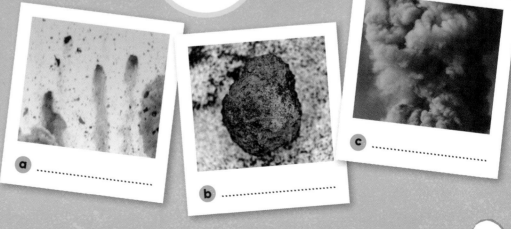

a ....

b ....

c ....

KRAKATAU

In May 1883, an island volcano in Indonesia called Krakatau started to spew out ash. Then, in August, it suddenly exploded in one of the biggest eruptions in history. It turned most of the island to dust, and the ash cloud rose 50 miles (80 km) into the sky.

THE KRAKATAU ERUPTION IS THE **LOUDEST** SOUND EVER RECORDED!

Krakatau erupting

Measuring eruptions

Volcano experts measure the size of eruptions using the Volcanic Explosivity Index (VEI). The higher the number, the bigger the eruption. Some examples can be seen below.

VEI 1
Gentle
Stromboli, Italy, Ongoing

VEI 4
Cataclysmic
Eyjafjallajökull, Iceland, 2010

VEI 6
Colossal
Krakatau, Indonesia, 1883

VEI 8
Mega-colossal
Yellowstone, US, 2 million years ago

DRAW THE BLAST

The largest-ever nuclear bomb exploded with the same power as 63 million tons (57 million metric tons) of TNT explosive. The Krakatau blast was more than three times bigger—equivalent to 220 million tons (200 million metric tons) of TNT. Count the number of squares in the nuclear blast below, then color in three times more squares around Krakatau.

DRAW IT!

KRAKATAU

THE BIGGEST NUCLEAR BLAST

RE-CREATE THE ISLAND

Almost three-quarters of the main Krakatau island disappeared in the 1883 eruption. The map below shows the islands as they are today. Plot the coordinates shown on the right. Then, join all the points to show the outline of the original island. Don't forget to color it in!

Mark these coordinates on the grid:

(K,6) (K,7) (J,8) (K,9) (K,10) (J,10)

(J,11) (K,11) (L,12) (M,11) (M,10) (N,10)

(O,10) (O,9) (O,8) (P,7)

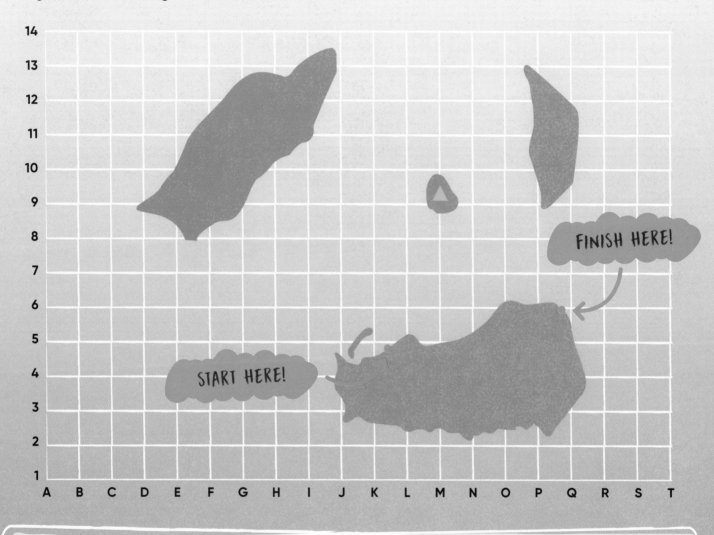

START HERE!

FINISH HERE!

MATCH THE MAPS

Krakatau and the islands nearby have changed drastically over time. Can you match each of these descriptions to the correct map? The triangles represent the volcanoes on the island.

MATCH IT!

1880
Krakatau is a large island, with a number of volcanoes.

1883
A huge explosion blasts away three-quarters of the main island.

1927
A new island volcano, Anak Krakatau (Child of Krakatau) emerges.

45

IT'S GONNA BLOW!

Scientists who study volcanoes are called volcanologists. Alongside other tasks, they have the exciting job of going up close to volcanoes—the information they collect helps predict whether the volcano will erupt.

DRAW THE TOOLS
Read the information in the tools panel and use the clues to help you figure out which objects are missing here. Then, draw them in.

A camera that can see how hot things are

A tool for collecting lava

A volcanologist's tools
Volcanologists use a range of types of equipment—some simple, some high-tech.

Satellites
From high up in the sky, satellites make detailed maps to show where lava might flow next.

Tiltmeter
This device detects when the ground tilts because a volcano is bulging with magma and gas.

Thermal imaging camera
This gadget sees heat and can be used to check whether parts of the ground are getting warmer as magma builds up.

Heat suit
This metal-coated suit reflects the heat of lava, keeping the volcanologist inside cool.

Hot rod
This long metal stick is used to collect samples of lava for study.

Thermocouple
This is an electrical thermometer that works at very high temperatures.

CHOOSE THE ALERT LEVEL
Use the information below to help you fill in the alert levels for these volcanoes (you'll only use three). Then, use the alert color to complete the border of each card.

NORMAL ▲ The volcano is not erupting and is very quiet.

ADVISORY ▲ The volcano appears to be more active than normal but is not erupting.

WATCH ▲ The volcano is growing more active, or a small eruption is already happening.

WARNING ▲ A big eruption of lava is very likely to happen soon or is already happening.

An eye in the sky with a great view of the ground below

An outfit that protects against extreme heat

DRAW IT!

A tool that detects if the ground tilts

A device for measuring temperature

A VOLCANOLOGIST'S **SUIT CAN WITHSTAND** TEMPERATURES OF **3,002°F** (1,650°C).

KILAUEA

LOCATION: Hawaii

TYPE: Shield volcano

ALERT LEVEL: ....

KARYMSKY

LOCATION: Russia

TYPE: Stratovolcano

ALERT LEVEL: ....

PARINACOTA

LOCATION: Bolivia

TYPE: Stratovolcano

ALERT LEVEL: ....

COLOR IT!

ROBOTS

Eruptions are very dangerous. As well as heat and explosions, they may also produce poisonous gases. Robots can get a good look at erupting volcanoes that are too dangerous for humans. Scientists send robots to take pictures and measurements. Small robots can go into areas, like lava tubes, where humans cannot fit.

WHICH ROBOT?

Read the descriptions of what these robots can do and then draw lines out of the lava tube maze to the correct robot.

Dante II
This walking robot can clamber over rocks that would block wheeled machines. A human controller operates it from a safer place, using a very long wire.

Research drone
Drones fitted with powerful cameras can give us a good view of volcanoes from above. They can also be flown into craters that would be impossible to climb inside.

a
It uses three caterpillar tracks to roll over lava flows and can stomp up and down to walk over rocks.

b
Built to explore volcanoes on other planets, this robot is small enough to roll through lava tubes.

START HERE!

c
This remote-controlled machine can fly over volcanoes to take pictures and record videos.

d
It uses spiderlike long legs to walk over rocky ground and take measurements.

TrackWalker II
This little tanklike robot trundles along on three caterpillar tracks. It can also lift up the tracks like feet so it can walk over rough ground.

VolcanoBot 1
This little rolling explorer fits inside caves and lava tubes. It was made by American space scientists who wanted a machine to explore volcanoes on other planets!

a ....

b ....

c ....

d ....

NAME THE VOLCANOES
Drones can fly over volcanoes to see when they might erupt and monitor them during eruptions. Can you identify each of these images taken by drones, using the descriptions to help you?

Mount Semeru, Indonesia
A cloud of ash billows from the crater during an eruption. The ash would choke a person who got too close.

FILL IT IN!

Mount Bromo, Indonesia
A lake of water steams inside the crater. The chemicals mixed in make the water green.

Mount Nyiragongo, Democratic Republic of the Congo
A deep lake of lava bubbles away inside the crater.

Mount Fagradalsfjall, Iceland
Molten lava flows out of the crater and forms a red-hot river flowing downhill.

DESIGN YOUR OWN ROBOT
Can you invent a new kind of robot to investigate volcanoes? Draw your design here. The robot explorer needs to be able to complete these jobs:

1. It must climb steep slopes, cross rough ground, and fly over lava.

2. It will need to take measurements with cameras, gas detectors, and thermometers.

3. It must collect rocks and lava samples so they can be studied in a laboratory. How will the robot pick these up, and where will it keep them? Remember, some samples will be hot!

DRAW IT!

IS IT ACTIVE?

The world's volcanoes are divided into three categories: active, dormant, and extinct. Active volcanoes will erupt again one day, although we don't know exactly when. Dormant volcanoes have not erupted for many hundreds of years but might become active again in the future. Extinct volcanoes will never erupt again.

COLOR IN THE VOLCANOES

Use the information in the volcano life cycle panel to help you color in the insides of these volcanoes. They will show what happens inside a volcano at each stage of its life. Once the insides are complete, color in the ash cloud above the active volcano.

Volcano life cycle

A volcano forms where liquid rock reaches Earth's surface. As the volcano gets older, the magma inside it begins to cool down and solidify.

Active
Magma frequently rises up inside the volcano, and it erupts from time to time.

Dormant
The volcano hasn't erupted for thousands of years, but some magma is still present.

Extinct
The magma has completely solidified. It will not erupt again.

COLOR IT!

DRAW IT!

THERE ARE AROUND
1,350
ACTIVE
VOLCANOES
ON EARTH.

ACTIVE

The mountain shape of a volcano forms from many layers of hardened lava.

DORMANT

ACTIVE, DORMANT, OR EXTINCT?

Here are some different volcanoes. Decide whether each volcano is active, dormant, or extinct and then use the key to color in the white circles.

Coloring key

- Active
- Dormant
- Extinct

Tall volcanoes might have had many small eruptions or just a few very big ones.

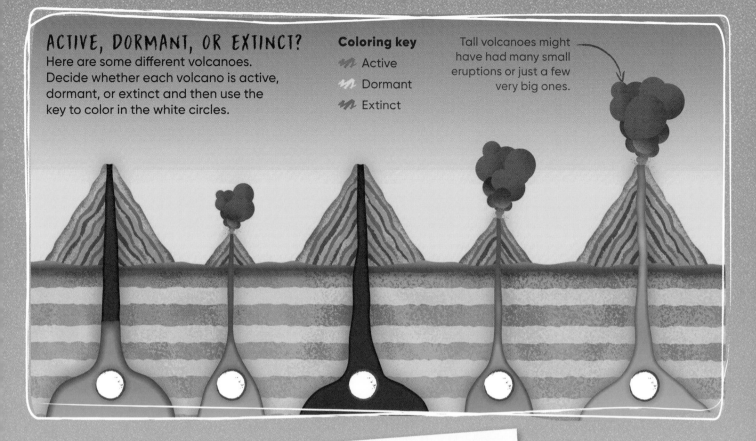

WILL IT ERUPT?

Read the descriptions of these volcanoes. Then, write **active**, **dormant**, or **extinct** in the spaces below the descriptions to show which stage of its life cycle each volcano is in.

COMPLETE IT!

Mount Fuji, Japan
It last erupted in 1707 but causes several small earthquakes every month.

....

Ben Nevis, UK
It last erupted 350 million years ago and has been slowly worn away since then.

....

Mount Kilimanjaro, Tanzania
It last erupted 200,000 years ago but caused earthquakes 200 years ago.

....

EXTINCT

VOLCANOES AND THE CLIMATE

Volcanic eruptions can be so huge that they change the climate all over the planet. Eruptions also generate their own weather, such as lightning within an ash cloud. When volcanic ash and gas mix with rain clouds, they can create acid rain, which contains chemicals that erode rocks, kill plants, and contaminate rivers and lakes.

Changing the climate
Clouds of ash and gas from an eruption rise high into the air and are blown around the globe. Gas forms aerosol particles that block the sun's rays, so temperatures on the ground get cooler—these can stay in the stratosphere for years.

COLOR THE ASH CLOUD
In 1991, the eruption of Mount Pinatubo in the Philippines released around 22 million tons (20 million metric tons) of gas and ash into the air. This cloud circled the globe for three weeks, blocking out sunlight and creating wintry weather. Use the key to help you color in the map to show how different areas were affected.

IN 1815, ASH FROM **MOUNT TAMBORA, INDONESIA,** MADE THE WORLD **1°F (0.5°C) COLDER** FOR A YEAR.

Mount Pinatubo

COLOR IT!

Coloring key
1 High levels of ash
2 Medium levels of ash
3 Low levels of ash

Mount Pinatubo today

LIGHT UP THE CLOUDS

As clouds of ash and gas swirl above a volcano, different sections rub against each other. This creates powerful lightning storms, which can cause fires and electrical surges on the ground. Join the dots to make two bolts of lightning inside this ash cloud.

Volcanic lightning at Taal Volcano, Philippines

START HERE!

FINISH HERE!

GET THROUGH THE ASH

Ash clouds can be dangerous for aircraft. Hard grains of ash scratch windows, making it difficult for pilots to see. The ash can also be sucked into engines, causing them to stop. Draw a path to guide this plane safely through the ash-cloud maze.

COLD **WEATHER** CREATED BY AN **ERUPTION** IS CALLED A **VOLCANIC WINTER.**

AFTER THE ERUPTION

Even though volcanoes are dangerous to be around, many people still choose to live near them. This is partly because the deposits from eruptions can develop fertile soil that contains key nutrients. Right after an eruption, the landscape looks lifeless, but animals, plants, and people begin to return very soon.

60 MILLION PEOPLE LIVE WITHIN 6.2 MILES (10 KM) OF AN ACTIVE VOLCANO.

New life

The first plants to grow on cooled lava are often ferns. When the ferns die, their dead leaves and stalks rot into the soil and nourish other plants.

Ferns do not grow flowers or fruits. They have feathery leaves called fronds.

FIND THE NUTRIENTS

Volcanic ash is full of nutrients that plants can use to help them grow. Some of these nutrients are below. Look up, down, left, right, and diagonally in the grid to find them.

B	S	I	W	F	K	B	I	F	R	H	W	I
T	J	T	J	D	J	R	R	B	M	E	J	G
Y	L	F	Y	P	U	O	M	M	U	I	P	I
J	M	O	W	H	B	G	P	R	Y	O	H	E
I	V	E	P	N	L	Z	C	M	T	S	O	Q
T	R	L	J	S	Z	O	X	A	C	Q	S	T
S	U	O	T	O	X	P	S	T	X	K	P	Z
U	B	H	N	H	T	S	O	R	W	E	H	N
L	A	M	B	P	I	P	D	V	H	F	O	A
F	A	U	I	U	H	C	D	Q	S	C	R	A
U	X	W	M	M	A	G	N	E	S	I	U	M
R	I	G	H	S	V	U	G	D	Y	Y	S	J
T	R	D	K	G	P	T	A	R	Y	E	F	A

Iron   Potassium   Sulfur   Phosphorus   Magnesium

IT TAKES ABOUT 150 YEARS FOR A LAVA FIELD TO TURN INTO A FULL FOREST.

COMPLETE THE TIMELINE

Put these post-eruption images in order by writing the letter of each image in its correct place on the timeline.

FILL IT IN!

DAY 1 ..... 1 YEAR LATER ..... 10 YEARS LATER ..... 20 YEARS LATER .....

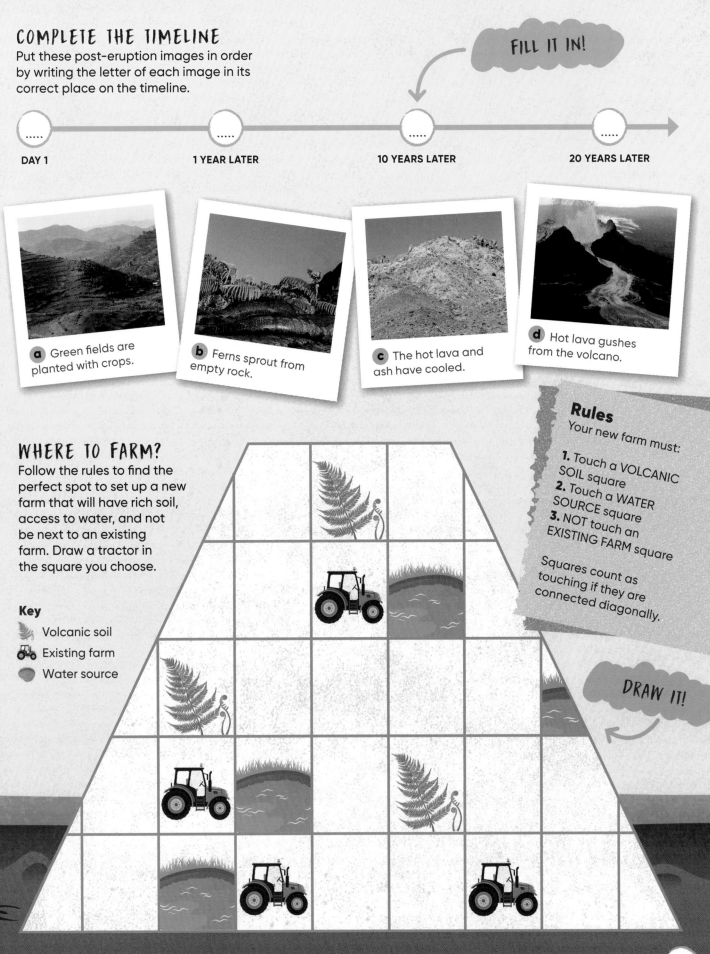

a Green fields are planted with crops.

b Ferns sprout from empty rock.

c The hot lava and ash have cooled.

d Hot lava gushes from the volcano.

WHERE TO FARM?

Follow the rules to find the perfect spot to set up a new farm that will have rich soil, access to water, and not be next to an existing farm. Draw a tractor in the square you choose.

Key
- Volcanic soil
- Existing farm
- Water source

Rules

Your new farm must:

1. Touch a VOLCANIC SOIL square
2. Touch a WATER SOURCE square
3. NOT touch an EXISTING FARM square

Squares count as touching if they are connected diagonally.

DRAW IT!

POMPEII

The Roman city of Pompeii was located at the foot of Mount Vesuvius in Italy. In 79 CE, this big volcano erupted suddenly, covering the city in a thick layer of hot ash. The city lay buried for centuries until archaeologists began to dig away the ash. They found the city just as it was on the day of the eruption.

Mount Vesuvius

Vesuvius is a stratovolcano on the western coast of Italy, near the modern city of Naples. It is still active today and last erupted in 1944.

DRAW IT!

FINISH THE MOSAIC

The Romans decorated their floors and walls with mosaics—pictures made from squares of colored tiles cemented into a pattern. Using the tiles on the left to help you, color the gaps in this mosaic of Vesuvius. This kind of eruption is called Plinian because it was first described by Roman writer Pliny the Younger, who witnessed the 79 CE eruption.

DRAW IT!

WHAT HAPPENED?

The eruption of Vesuvius started slowly, and the townspeople of Pompeii were unconcerned. However, things got very bad very quickly. Read the timeline to find out what happened and then draw a picture of each stage of the eruption.

VESUVIUS HAS **ERUPTED** AROUND **36 TIMES** SINCE 79 CE.

A tall ash cloud appears above Vesuvius.

Ash begins to rain down upon Pompeii, blanketing the streets. The air gets warmer.

12pm

2pm

WHICH IS WHICH?

The volcanic ash froze Pompeii in time. Lava and ash hardened around the victims of the volcano, becoming rock, and gaps were left in this rock as the bodies rotted away. Thousands of years later, archaeologists poured plaster into the gaps, creating casts. Other items were burned into solid carbon. Draw a line to match these Pompeiian objects with their descriptions.

IT ONLY TOOK **45 MINUTES** FOR ALL OF **POMPEII** TO BE **BURIED IN** ASH AND ROCK.

a

b

c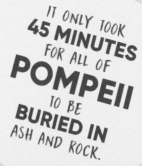

d

e

Dog
A cast of a pet dog that was caught in the eruption

Loaf of bread
A round loaf of bread fresh from the oven, which is now solid carbon

Bronze Medusa
A metal object showing the mythical Medusa, a woman with snakes for hair

Mosaic
A picture of a dog made from lots of small, colored tiles

Glass jar
A jar that may have been used for medicine or special foods and sauces

MATCH IT!

Rocks thrown from the volcano fall down on the city, and roofs begin to collapse under the weight of the ash.

People try to escape the city but cannot find their way because the sun is blocked out by the ash.

A pyroclastic flow begins to erupt from Vesuvius and flows downhill toward Pompeii.

It's all over. The buildings and people of Pompeii have been buried under a thick layer of ash.

5pm   5:30pm   11:15pm   12am

Useful volcanoes

Although volcanic eruptions can be destructive, they also provide rare and useful resources. This includes everything from diamonds and precious metals, like gold, to fertile farming land and sources of energy.

Fertile soil
The soil around a volcano is enriched by ash released during eruptions. It is full of minerals needed to grow healthy crops.

Diamonds
Gemstones such as diamonds were brought up from inside Earth by kimberlite eruptions, last seen about 25 million years ago.

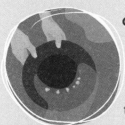

Gold
Precious metals like gold are more common when volcanoes heat the water inside rocks. Particles of gold are deposited into fractures called veins.

Beautiful landscapes
Volcanoes create stunning natural features that attract tourists. More than one million people visit Mount Fuji in Japan every year.

Geothermal energy
The heat from a volcano can be used to create electricity and hot water for local people.

VOLCANIC BENEFITS

Although active volcanoes can be dangerous, they can also benefit the environment and local economy. Volcanoes are amazing places to visit, but many people also live near volcanoes, working on farms around them and even in mines deep down in the hot Earth.

FIND THE DIAMONDS
The hardest natural substance in the world, diamonds are gemstones made deep in Earth's mantle. Using the coloring key, color in this crystal to reveal the diamonds.

Coloring key

How many blue diamonds did you find?

.....

COLOR IT!

WHO'S WHO?

Read the postcards below and determine which picture shows which traveler. Draw a line between the matching photo and postcard.

MATCH IT!

a

b

c

Dear Mom and Dad,
I'm having a great trip near Mount Nyiragongo in the Democratic Republic of the Congo. I'm looking forward to a fruity breakfast!

From Violet

Dear Granny,
My friends and I found this amazing piece of gold ore in some rocks near the Mount Galeras volcano in Colombia!

See you soon, Kemi

Dear Aunty,
Here I am in front of Mount Etna in Italy. People have been growing grapes here for thousands of years!

Love, Alex

WRITE IT!

LABEL THE PLANT

At a geothermal plant, cold water is pumped down into hot rocks. As the water heats up and becomes steam, it rises up through a pipe to the surface, where it spins a turbine inside a generator, which creates electricity. Use the words below to complete the labels on this diagram of a geothermal plant.

a ....

b ....

c ....

d ....

e ....

Steam   Water

Pump

Hot rocks   Generator

VOLCANIC WILDLIFE

Once the eruptions are over, volcanoes can become homes to some amazing wildlife. Plants are able to grow rapidly from cracks in cooled lava or volcanic ash deposits as soils form there. Some animals have adapted to use the heat and chemicals from volcanoes to help them stay alive.

LIKE HUMANS, **JAPANESE MACAQUES** CAN DEVELOP **DIFFERENT ACCENTS** DEPENDING ON WHERE THEY LIVE.

FIND THE PATH

Japanese macaques live in cold forests, eating whatever they can find. When the winter snows come, these monkeys need to find a warm place to relax. Can you help this macaque find a path to the volcanic spring? (Hint: There is more than one path.)

In autumn, the monkeys grow thick fur to keep out the cold.

During winter, the only food around for the monkeys is pine needles and bark.

START HERE

CHOOSE THE BEST NEST

This Galápagos land iguana needs to lay its eggs in a warm, sandy place near a volcano. Read the descriptions below and then choose which would be the best place for a nest.

- **a** Another iguana already nesting
- **b** Deep down a very steep slope inside the volcano
- **c** Cozy hot sand on top of a crater
- **d** On a rocky cliff

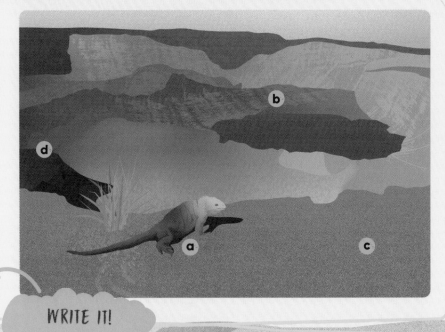

....

WRITE IT!

FINISH HERE

As the weather gets colder, most monkeys start walking south, where it is warmer.

Some monkeys stay warm in the snow by sitting in warm volcanic springs.

FIND THE WORD

Tardigrades (also called water bears) are micro-animals that can live in extreme places that would kill other creatures. Use the vowels from the letters below to fill in the blanks and discover the word for these types of animals.

EDWHEPQFVCONBITYSE

_xtr_m_ph_l_s

GUESS WHO?

Volcanic lakes are filled with chemicals that would kill most wildlife. However, a type of algae can survive there, and one bird species can wade in these lakes. Read these four descriptions of birds and write down which one you think lives near a volcano.

....

Lake Natron, Tanzania

Flamingo
This wading bird eats algae, which makes its feathers pink.

African fish eagle
This hunting bird catches fish from rivers and lakes.

Yellow-billed stork
This bird uses its long beak to snap up fish in shallow water.

Gray-crowned crane
Feeding mostly on land for insects, this bird lives in the wetlands.

61

ICY VOLCANOES

Although volcanoes are incredibly hot, they can form in the coldest parts of the world. Many volcanoes lie under glaciers or layers of snow and ice in places such as Antarctica and Iceland. When these volcanoes erupt, the lava melts the ice.

MATCH THE FACTS

Antarctica is almost completely covered in thick ice but is home to 90 volcanoes. Here are some facts about three of them. Use what you learn to answer the quiz below.

Eruption under a glacier

A glacier is a large area of slow-moving ice. When lava erupts from a volcano under a glacier, it melts the ice above it. The melted ice cools the lava, forming tubes and balls of rock called pillow lava.

A cloud of steam rises above the hidden volcano.

Glacier

Melted ice flows away under the glacier.

The mountain is made of pillow lava from previous eruptions.

MOUNT EREBUS

LOCATION:	Ross Island
TYPE:	Stratovolcano
HEIGHT:	12,448 ft (3,794 m)
ACTIVITY:	Frequently erupts

MOUNT TERROR

LOCATION:	Ross Island
TYPE:	Shield volcano
HEIGHT:	10,702 ft (3,262 m)
ACTIVITY:	Last erupted more than 11,700 years ago

MOUNT MELBOURNE

LOCATION:	Coast of Antarctica
TYPE:	Stratovolcano
HEIGHT:	8,963 ft (2,732 m)
ACTIVITY:	Last erupted between 1862 and 1922

a The most active volcano is:

- ☐ Mount Erebus
- ☐ Mount Terror
- ☐ Mount Melbourne

b This volcano is not on an island:

- ☐ Mount Erebus
- ☐ Mount Terror
- ☐ Mount Melbourne

c This volcano is taller than the others:

- ☐ Mount Erebus
- ☐ Mount Terror
- ☐ Mount Melbourne

d This volcano is not a stratovolcano:

- ☐ Mount Erebus
- ☐ Mount Terror
- ☐ Mount Melbourne

FIND MOUNT EREBUS

Mount Erebus is the southernmost active volcano on Earth. Mark its location on the map by following the instructions on the right.

Route

Travel by sled six squares south.
Travel by sled four squares west.
Travel by boat two squares south.
Draw Mount Erebus in the square.
Find the square's coordinates and write them in the box.

┌─────────┐
│ _ _   │
└─────────┘

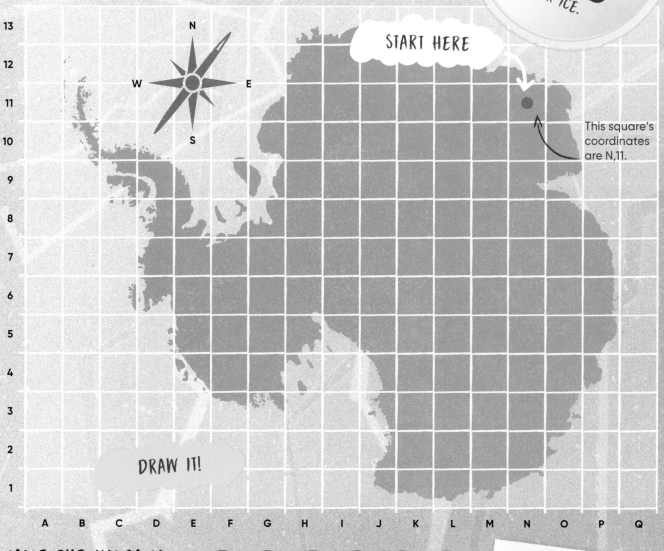

START HERE

This square's coordinates are N,11.

DRAW IT!

13 12 11 10 9 8 7 6 5 4 3 2 1

A B C D E F G H I J K L M N O P Q

NAME THE VOLCANO

Antarctica's most active volcano is covered in fumaroles that melt the ice above. These are also called snow chimneys. To reveal the volcano's name, cross out the letters in SNOW CHIMNEY and then rearrange the remaining letters.

┌──────────────────┐
│ _ _ _ _ _ _ _   │
└──────────────────┘

N E S E W H
C B O M U E
N Y I R S

Fumaroles are holes in Earth's surface that vent steam.

63

SPACE VOLCANOES

As well as on Earth, volcanoes occur on the surface of other planets and moons. The biggest volcano that we know of is Olympus Mons, on Mars. Some planets and moons have no active volcanoes but are covered in rock from past eruptions. Some planets' moons have cryovolcanoes (ice volcanoes), which erupt slushy ice instead of magma.

Space probes
We can't visit other planets to see their volcanoes, so we send space probes. These robotic spacecraft, such as NASA's *New Horizons*, shown here, are controlled from Earth. The probes send back photos for scientists to study.

Solar System
Our sun is orbited by eight planets, including Earth. Some of these planets have moons that orbit them. This collection of planets and moons is called the solar system.

THE SUN

MERCURY

VENUS

EARTH

MARS

Rocky planets
The four planets closest to the sun, which include Earth, are formed of rock.

WHICH VOLCANO IS WHERE?
Read the clues under the images to help you figure out where in the solar system these volcanoes can be found.

WRITE IT!

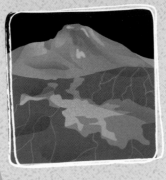

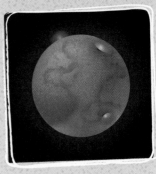

a ....
The second planet from the sun is almost completely covered in thousands of volcanoes.

b ....
The surface of this red planet is covered in giant volcanoes, each hundreds of miles wide.

c ....
There are hundreds of active volcanoes on Io, a moon orbiting the largest gas giant.

Olympus Mons

The planet Mars is home to the largest volcano in our solar system, Olympus Mons. It covers 116,000 sq miles (300,000 sq km) and has been erupting for two billion years!

HOW BIG IS THE VOLCANO?

The island country of Vanuatu spans more than 4,600 sq miles (12,000 sq km). It is shown as a yellow box below. Color 25 squares in the second grid to see how much bigger Olympus Mons is.

COLOR IT!

JUPITER

SATURN

URANUS

NEPTUNE

Gas giants
The four planets farthest from the sun are massive balls of swirling gas.

d ....
Volcanoes once erupted all over the sun's closest neighbor but have been dormant for 3.5 billion years.

e ....
Icy cryovolcanoes cover Enceladus, which is a moon of this gas giant with spectacular rings.

f ....
On Triton, the largest moon of this planet that is farthest from the sun, geysers spurt out dust and nitrogen gas.

ERUPTIONS **ON IO,** ONE OF JUPITER'S MOONS, CAN REACH **300 MILES** (480 KM) HIGH!

VOLCANIC LANDFORMS

Magma from volcanic activity can leave behind very distinctive rock formations. Sometimes, the magma has cooled underground, and the land above is worn away to reveal it. Other times, it erupts out of the ground and cools on the surface.

BALL'S PYRAMID IN THE PACIFIC OCEAN IS THE WORLD'S TALLEST VOLCANIC PLUG AT 1,844 FT (562 M) TALL.

Rock formations
Hot magma can force its way up through, or between, rock layers. If it collects in a large space, it may even push the ground up to form a hill or mountain.

Cooled lava field
This landform has been formed by cooled lava from an active volcano.

Laccolith
This dome-shaped feature is made by magma pushing the ground up.

Exposed batholith
This large, underground magma pool was revealed as the land above it eroded away.

Ring dike
This is a ring of spikes and walls where a volcanic crater and eruption pipe used to be.

Volcanic plug
This is magma that has cooled inside a volcano's vent, blocking it. The rest has worn away.

Sill
This forms when magma flows into horizontal cracks underground and cools.

Dike
This is where magma pushes up vertically through rock layers and cools.

FIND THE FORMATIONS
How many words about volcanic landforms can you find in this wordsearch?

FIND IT!

Magma
Plug
Batholith
Sill
Laccolith
Volcano
Dike

```
        I F E
      D R B M U C   D V B E R
  M A G M A S I V E Y F E P W F Y G I
  K I S E X D K L L A C C O L I T H S
  W E I O C U E R B O S R J V U O M L
  A L L S G I P Q U W P N O K E G W I
  J Y L V M E B A T H O L I T H I U C
  M H A F R O H J T E V O N A C L O V
```

Sugar Loaf Mountain, Brazil

Tall domes of rock that are left over from magma chambers that cooled underground.

WHAT AM I? ....

EXTRUSIVE OR INTRUSIVE?

Magma that breaks the surface and cools quickly there becomes "extrusive" igneous rock. Magma that cools slowly underground forms "intrusive" igneous rock. Label the **intrusive** and **extrusive** rocks on this diagram.

a ....

b ....

NAME THAT FEATURE

Using what you have learned about the rock features left behind by cooled magma, can you figure out what these famous landmarks are made from? Read the descriptions and write the answers in the spaces provided.

Pilanesberg, South Africa

A circle of walls and spikelike rocks that surround where a crater used to be.

WHAT AM I? ....

Ship Rock, US

A tall spike-shaped rock that formed as magma cooled within a now extinct volcano.

WHAT AM I? ....

HOW DID IT LOOK?

On the right is a volcanic plug that formed long ago. Draw what it might have looked like millions of years ago, before the magma cooled and the layers of softer rocks eroded away. To help you, here are some clues:

1. The plug was once molten and connected to a magma chamber.

2. The plug filled the vent where magma escaped from the volcano. There was once a whole mountain around it, which has since worn away.

DRAW IT!

HOT SPRINGS AND GEYSERS

Deep underground, water heats up as it trickles through hot, volcanic rock. When the water reaches the surface, it erupts as hot springs, geysers, and other features. Colorful bacteria and microbes are the only living things that can survive such extreme heat.

Fly Ranch
In Nevada, the Fly Ranch Geyser was made by accident in 1916 by a farmer drilling for water. Over time, minerals in the water have created colorful mounds.

Geothermal features
The high pressure that exists deep beneath the ground means water can be super-heated beyond its normal boiling point by the magma. This water comes to the surface in different ways, called geothermal features.

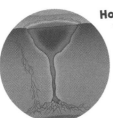

Hot spring
Hot water that can easily escape to the surface fills a pond or lake, which is called a hot spring.

Geyser
An underground spring boils and cools in a repeating pattern. Every so often, a jet of hot water squirts out of the ground.

Mud pot
Underground water boils and turns to steam. As it moves upward, the steam turns rock into hot, bubbling mud.

Fumarole
Steam escapes into the air along a crack in the rock. Solidifying minerals also create a rocky spout on the surface.

SKETCH THE SCENE
Hot volcanic water contains different minerals, dissolved from rocks as the scalding water passes through them. Above ground, the water cools and the minerals solidify into colorful crystals. Over time, the crystals build up into mounds. Draw jets of hot water and steam coming out of this mound.

DRAW IT!

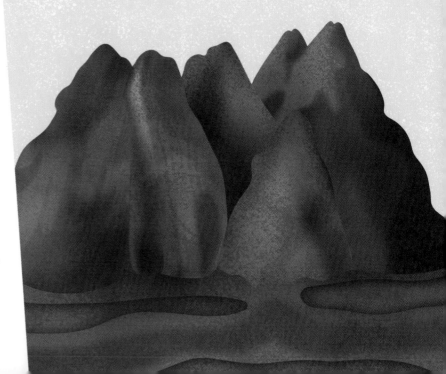

FIGURE OUT THE FEATURE

Read the clues to work out which type of geothermal feature is in each square. Add the correct labels and then draw pictures of them.

Hot spring   Fumarole

Geyser   Mud pot

DRAW IT!

a ....
The water turns to steam and bubbles up through mud.

b ....
Hot water and steam erupt regularly from an underground spring.

c ....
This lake is fed by a constant supply of hot water.

d ....
Steam forms under the ground and escapes through a crack in the rock.

COLOR THE HOT SPRING

Some hot springs contain brightly colored microbes that feed on the minerals in the water. Toward the edges, the water is cooler, and more microbe species are able to survive. Use the coloring key to color in this hot spring.

STEAMBOAT GEYSER IN YELLOWSTONE IS THE WORLD'S TALLEST GEYSER, AT **300 FT (91 M).**

Coloring key

1 **Boiling:** no microbes

2 **Very hot:** *Synechococcus* bacteria

3 **Hot:** *Synechococcus* and *Chloroflexus* bacteria

4 **Warm:** a mixture of microbes, including *Deinococcus-Thermus*

COLOR IT!

69

YELLOWSTONE

Yellowstone is a beautiful national park in Wyoming. It is home to spectacular volcanic features, such as hot springs, boiling mud pools, and natural fountains called geysers. The park sits on a colossal "supervolcano," which could erupt again one day—although it is unlikely to happen for tens of thousands of years.

THE LAST BIG **ERUPTION** AT YELLOWSTONE WAS **640,000** YEARS AGO.

Minerva Terrace

Grand Prismatic Spring

Yellowstone Lake

Castle Geyser

Old Faithful

Red Spouter

Yellowstone Caldera

Hidden under the national park is a huge volcanic crater—the Yellowstone Caldera. The caldera is a supervolcano. Its magma makes the land above it bulge, causing frequent earthquakes. The caldera's heat creates volcanic features, such as hot springs and geysers.

The Yellowstone Caldera is around 43 miles (70 km) wide.

COLOR THE ASH

If the Yellowstone supervolcano erupts, the explosion and deposits will destroy the national park and cover much of North America in ash. Use the key colors to complete this map showing what would happen in different areas.

COLOR IT!

Coloring key

1 Raining ash

2 Heavy ash fall

3 Total destruction

WHICH IS WHICH?

Yellowstone is full of volcanic features—here are just a few of them. Read the descriptions of the features given below and then write in the correct name under each picture on the right.

a ....

b ....

c ....

d ....

e ....

WRITE IT!

Yellowstone Lake
A large lake that partly fills the Yellowstone Caldera

Grand Prismatic Spring
A hot spring with rings of brightly colored rocks and microorganisms

Castle Geyser
A natural fountain that sends up bursts of water from time to time

Red Spouter
A pool of hot, red mud that bubbles and steams as gases escape

Minerva Terrace
A staircase of limestone formed by trickles of hot volcanic water

NAME THE GEYSER

The most famous geyser at Yellowstone is known for erupting a fountain of water every hour or so. Each eruption lasts for a few minutes. Find this geyser's name by unscrambling the letters that are floating in it.

H O D A I T F L F U L

The water from this geyser reaches heights of up to 180 ft (55 m).

_ _ _   _ _ _ _ _ _

THE OCEAN FLOOR

Most of the volcanic eruptions on Earth are happening under the sea. Lava erupts from vents on the seafloor, and the flows form entire mountain ranges underwater. These submarine volcanoes can grow tall enough to become whole new islands above the water's surface.

THREE-QUARTERS OF THE WORLD'S LAVA ERUPTS FROM MID-OCEAN RIDGES.

Undersea volcanoes

Much of the volcanic activity on the ocean floor is caused by the movement of Earth's tectonic plates. As the plates shift, magma moves with them and can make its way to the surface, forming a range of volcanic features.

1 Guyot
This is an extinct underwater volcano with a flat top.

2 Mid-ocean ridge
Lava rises between tectonic plates as they pull apart, forming mountain ranges.

3 Seamount
This is an underwater volcano that is either active or inactive.

4 Ocean trench
When one plate is pushed under another, a long, deep trench forms at the bottom of the ocean.

5 Volcanic island
When an underwater volcano grows above the water's surface, it becomes an island.

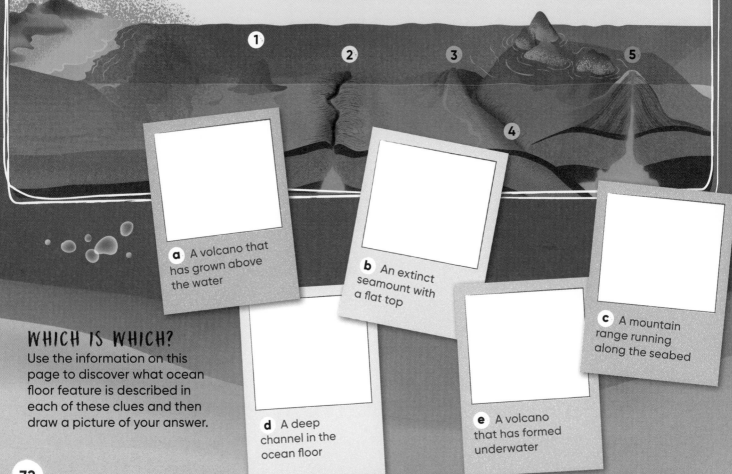

a A volcano that has grown above the water

b An extinct seamount with a flat top

c A mountain range running along the seabed

d A deep channel in the ocean floor

e A volcano that has formed underwater

WHICH IS WHICH?
Use the information on this page to discover what ocean floor feature is described in each of these clues and then draw a picture of your answer.

TRENCH OR RIDGE?

Trenches form where two tectonic plates push together. Ridges, on the other hand, form where the plates are pulled apart. Label these diagrams to show which one is a **trench** and which one is a **ridge**.

a ....

b ....

WRITE IT!

Deepest point

The Mariana Trench in the Pacific Ocean is the deepest place on Earth, reaching 36,201 ft (11,034 m) below sea level. This is deeper than Earth's highest point, Mount Everest, is tall! It was formed by the massive Pacific Plate pushing into and moving under the Philippine Plate.

FIND THE FEATURES

Can you unscramble these letters to spell out the names of five underwater volcanic features? Write your answers underneath each bubble.

G O Y U T

a ....

I C O M I E O R G E N D I D A D E

b ....

O R C E C A N T E H H N

c ....

O S E N M A T U

d ....

V I L L D A C I C O S N N A

e ....

73

DEEP-SEA VENTS

Volcanic hot springs on the seabed are called hydrothermal vents. They are also called "black smokers" because, when their super-hot water gushes into the cold sea, the chemicals in it crystallize into tiny specks that make the water dark and "smoky." Bacteria in seawater eat the chemicals from the vents, and many unusual animals live around them.

BUILD A VENT
Use what you have learned about hydrothermal vents to draw your own one here. There are some suggestions below. When you have finished, you could add some animals living around the vent.

1. Draw in the cracks and channels under the seabed first.

2. Now, color in the water. Don't forget that some of it is cold, some is hot, and some is dark and "smoky."

DRAW IT!

Undersea chimneys
Hydrothermal vents have "chimneys" rising up from the seabed —some are as high as a house. The chimneys grow even taller as the minerals that are mixed into the hot water are deposited, layer after layer.

The vent water is 752°F (400°C), while the seawater around it is almost freezing.

Hydrothermal vents are often found near undersea volcanoes.

Tube worms often live near vents and can grow up to 10 ft (3 m) long!

The cold water is warmed up as it flows through hot volcanic rocks.

The vent is supplied with cold seawater that trickles down through cracks.

MATCH THE DEEP DIVERS

The only way to see a vent on the ocean floor is in a submersible. The first to discover vents was *Alvin*, in 1977. Match the description of each submersible to its picture by drawing a line between them.

MATCH IT!

HROV Nereus
Designed to go to the deepest parts of the ocean, this uncrewed submersible is often operated via a long cable controlled by a human controller aboard a ship at the surface.

AUTOSUB600
Built to dive up to 19,685 ft (6,000 m), this torpedo-shaped robot explorer is designed to work without a human controller. It is given a mission and left to complete it.

Alvin
This three-person craft had powerful lights and mechanical pincers for grabbing objects on the seabed. *Alvin* was also used to explore the wreck of the *Titanic*.

a

b

c

X L I M P B W C N L J G B D S
B V A B I E S R Y Q Z A A T
I M N G M U N Y A M V C P M
B R B J A D V E B P T W I R L
V E F A S K E E R R E P M B O A A
H C H I M N E Y H R A T T B W Q D
R A L R O Q P V I T D L B T O L
Z Y F T K O G A A O O C F K O
M U H W E E H S V P P R Z I G
U H Y D R O T H E R M A L G
H I Y N E N T F U U
Z G D U T G Q C Z
P F B P P T N L M
V M

SEARCH BELOW
Search the grid for these words that are all related to deep-sea vents.

Hydrothermal	**Worm**	**Smoker**
Vent	**Mineral**	
Deep	**Chimney**	**Bacteria**

DRAW IT!

FIND THE ANIMALS
Many different animals live around the vents, although they stay away from the super-hot water jets. Read the descriptions under each circle and find that animal on these pages. Then, draw it in the circle.

Light shrimp
This pale shrimp has two glowing dots on its back.

Yeti crab
This hairy-looking crab has long pincers.

Pale octopus
This animal has eight sucker-covered tentacles.

VOLCANIC ISLANDS

Many of the world's volcanoes start on the seabed, slowly growing taller and taller. Some of them get tall enough to break through the surface of the water, forming an island. Nearly all the islands far out to sea were created this way, although their volcanoes may now be extinct.

FINISH THE PICTURE

Volcanic islands may look big, but they are just a tiny part of the whole volcano. Most of the rock is hidden underwater. Draw in the missing parts of this volcanic island.

Growing an island

Lava erupting on the seafloor cools down very fast. Its outer part becomes solid, but the inside is still liquid. Lava bursts out again, making fresh rocks that build up and become an island.

New volcano
A seabed volcano often forms where plates are pulling apart.

Seamount
A volcano that is entirely underwater is called a seamount.

Island tip
Eruptions pile up lava and rock until it breaks through the surface.

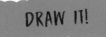

DRAW IT!

New island

The island of Surtsey rose south of Iceland during an eruption in 1963. Within a few years, plants and animals had made it their home.

COMPLETE IT!

CREATE AN ISLAND

Wildlife reaches new volcanic islands in three ways: it is blown by the wind, it floats there on a tree trunk or other natural raft, or it follows new ocean currents. Follow these steps to reveal the wildlife of Surtsey.

1. Join the dots to create the current outline of the island. The shape is still changing as waves wash parts away and new eruptions add land.

2. In the circles, draw the different types of life that have made it to the island over the years. Surtsey also has many mushrooms, which arrive as tiny spores mixed with rain.

Seeds
These are dropped by passing birds or may be carried by the wind.

Spiders
These creatures are thought to have drifted to Surtsey on the wind.

Tufts of grass
This plant matter provides mini-rafts for insects and seeds.

Birds
The island provides a useful resting place for birds.

MATCH IT!

WHICH IS WHICH?

An atoll is an island made from a ring of coral surrounding a lagoon. After a volcano becomes extinct, it breaks up and falls back into the sea, leaving the atoll behind. To see how this happens, match each picture to its caption.

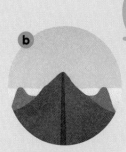

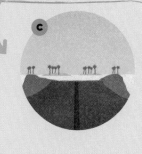

ICELAND IS THE WORLD'S LARGEST VOLCANIC ISLAND.

Sinking island
After the volcano stops erupting, it begins to sink, but the coral reef keeps growing.

Atoll and lagoon
The volcano has eroded into the sea. The coral reef creates a lagoon in its place.

Active volcano
A coral reef begins to form around the coast of a volcanic island that is still erupting.

UNIQUE VOLCANOES

Every volcano has its own unique set of incredible features, depending on its location, the type of rock it's made of, the way in which it was formed, and the frequency and size of its eruptions. Here are four of the most amazing volcanoes on Earth.

MOUNT NYIRAGONGO'S LAVA LAKE IS 1,969 FT (600 M) DEEP.

Natural wonders

These four volcanoes are one-off wonders of the world. One has a lake filled with lava, and another has lava covered in blue flames. The third volcano never seems to stop erupting and, lastly, there's a volcano shaped in an almost perfect cone.

MOUNT YASUR
Vanuatu

This volcano has been erupting nonstop since at least 1774.

TYPE OF VOLCANO:	Stratovolcano
TYPE OF ERUPTION:	Vulcanian
HEIGHT:	1,184 ft (361 m)
LAST ERUPTION:	Currently erupting

MOUNT NYIRAGONGO
Democratic Republic of the Congo

This highly active volcano is famous for the huge lake of liquid lava in its crater.

TYPE OF VOLCANO:	Stratovolcano
TYPE OF ERUPTION:	Hawaiian
HEIGHT:	11,385 ft (3,470 m)
LAST ERUPTION:	2021

QUIZ YOURSELF

It's time to test your knowledge about these four incredible volcanoes. Read all the facts on these pages before answering the questions below.

WHICH ONE?

a Which of the four volcanoes is the only one located in Africa?

- ☐ Mount Nyiragongo
- ☐ Kawah Ijen
- ☐ Mount Yasur
- ☐ Mayon Volcano

b Which gas is the main cause of Kawah Ijen's blue flames?

- ☐ Sulfur
- ☐ Oxygen
- ☐ Carbon dioxide
- ☐ Hydrogen

c What is the shape of Mayon Volcano in the Philippines?

- ☐ Cube
- ☐ Cone
- ☐ Doughnut
- ☐ Sphere

d In which year do experts think that Mount Yasur began erupting?

- ☐ 2021
- ☐ 1218
- ☐ 1538
- ☐ 1774

CREATE YOUR OWN!

What's your idea of an amazing volcano? Think of a name and create a fact card for it, with a picture of it erupting. These questions will help.

1. Which type of volcano is it? Stratovolcanoes are the tallest, but shield volcanoes are bigger.

2. How does it erupt? With a huge explosion or a burning river of lava?

NAME: ....

LOCATION: ....

DESCRIPTION: ....
....
....

TYPE OF VOLCANO: ....

TYPE OF ERUPTION: ....

HEIGHT: ....

FILL IT IN!

KAWAH IJEN
Indonesia

At night, this volcano is lit up by blue flames! This is caused by sulfuric gases escaping from cracks round the crater.

TYPE OF VOLCANO:	*Stratovolcano*
TYPE OF ERUPTION:	*Strombolian*
HEIGHT:	*9,085 ft (2,769 m)*
LAST ERUPTION:	*1999*

MAYON VOLCANO
Philippines

This volcano is almost a perfect cone shape and looks the same when you view it from any angle.

TYPE OF VOLCANO:	*Stratovolcano*
TYPE OF ERUPTION:	*Plinian*
HEIGHT:	*8,077 ft (2,462 m)*
LAST ERUPTION:	*2019*

WHERE IN THE WORLD?

Use the coordinates to find the locations of the four volcanoes. Draw different-colored triangles to mark each volcano on the map.

Key

▲ Mount Nyiragongo (J,5)

▲ Mayon Volcano (Q,6)

▲ Kawah Ijen (P,4)

▲ Mount Yasur (T,3)

VOLCANO QUIZ

Now you have a chance to test your volcano knowledge with this quiz. Take as long as you need to answer each question. You can look at earlier pages to find some clues if you need to. Have fun and good luck!

HOW DID YOU DO?

Once you have answered the questions, you can check your answers at the back of the book. How many did you get right?

12–17 Red-hot! You're an expert!

6–11 Don't let the pressure get to you!

0–5 Your knowledge seems to be dormant!

1 Which robot is used to explore inside small caves and lava tubes?

- **a** Dante II
- **b** Research drone
- **c** TrackWalker II
- **d** VolcanoBot 1

2 The Ring of Fire is another name for a big volcano in Africa with a very large and round crater.

- ☐ True
- ☐ False

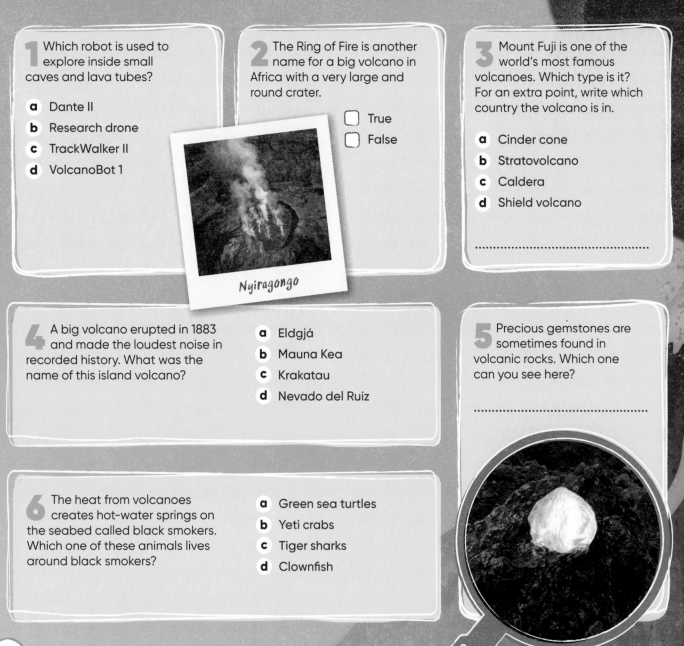

Nyiragongo

3 Mount Fuji is one of the world's most famous volcanoes. Which type is it? For an extra point, write which country the volcano is in.

- **a** Cinder cone
- **b** Stratovolcano
- **c** Caldera
- **d** Shield volcano

....

4 A big volcano erupted in 1883 and made the loudest noise in recorded history. What was the name of this island volcano?

- **a** Eldgjá
- **b** Mauna Kea
- **c** Krakatau
- **d** Nevado del Ruiz

5 Precious gemstones are sometimes found in volcanic rocks. Which one can you see here?

....

6 The heat from volcanoes creates hot-water springs on the seabed called black smokers. Which one of these animals lives around black smokers?

- **a** Green sea turtles
- **b** Yeti crabs
- **c** Tiger sharks
- **d** Clownfish

7 Igneous rocks are formed when magma and lava cool down. Which two rocks below are igneous?

a Pumice
b Limestone
c Basalt
d Marble

8 Known for their spectacular eruptions, which type of volcano system led to the formation of the Hawaiian islands?

a Ash pump
b Supervolcano
c Hotspot
d Rock spout

9 The largest volcano ever found is not on Earth. It is on the surface of Mars!

☐ True   ☐ False

10 Which of these is NOT a kind of lava seen erupting from volcanoes?

a Pillow
b Pahoehoe
c Eeek
d Aa

11 What is a volcano known as if it has not erupted for a long time?

....

12 What is the name given to a scientist who studies volcanoes?

....

13 What is the name of a swirling, fast-moving cloud of thick ash and gas from a volcano?

....

14 Which of these volcanoes destroyed the Roman city of Pompeii during an eruption in 79 CE?

a Olympus Mons
b Mount Vesuvius
c Mount Erebus
d Stromboli

15 What is a volcano called once it can never erupt again?

....

16 In 1916, a farmer in Nevada accidentally uncovered an underground geothermal feature known as what?

a Wasp Hill Spring
b Fly Ranch Geyser
c Insect Mudpot
d Spider Fumarole

VOLCANO!

Look around! There are volcanoes erupting, but also scientists and drones observing these amazing natural phenomena. Color in the picture and then draw some things you see in the panel on the right.

COLOR IT!

WHAT DO YOU SEE?
Find the five things listed below and draw them in the boxes.

DRAW IT!

Volcanologist

Shield volcano

Stratovolcano

Pyramid-shaped building

Research drone

RECORD BREAKERS

Volcanoes and earthquakes can be spectacular, destructive, and terrifying. Find out more about some of these record-breaking natural disasters.

Biggest eruptions

Here are the largest eruptions since the year 1000, based on the volume of material ejected in cubic miles (cubic kilometers).

MOUNT TAMBORA, INDONESIA, 1815
36 MILES³
(150 KM³)

KOLUMBO, GREECE, 1650
14.4 MILES³
(60 KM³)

KUWAE, VANUATU, 1452-53
8 MILES³
(33 KM³)

LONG ISLAND, PAPUA NEW GUINEA, 1660
7.2 MILES³
(30 KM³)

KRAKATAU, INDONESIA, 1883
5 MILES³
(21 KM³)

HUAYNAPUTINA, PERU, 1600
7.2 MILES³
(30 KM³)

Longest-lasting eruptions

Some volcanic eruptions don't just go on for days but last for years, or even centuries!

- 42 — ARENAL, COSTA RICA
- 49* — EREBUS, ANTARCTICA
- 50 — NYIRAGONGO, DR CONGO
- 55* — ERTA ALE, ETHIOPIA
- 61 — AIRA, JAPAN
- 77 — SANGAY, ECUADOR
- 88* — STROMBOLI, ITALY
- 89* — DUKONO, INDONESIA
- 100* — SANTA MARÍA, GUATEMALA
- YASUR, VANUATU — 297*

LENGTH OF ERUPTION IN YEARS   *(continuing)

Most volcanoes

These are the countries with the most volcanoes that have erupted in the last 12,000 years.

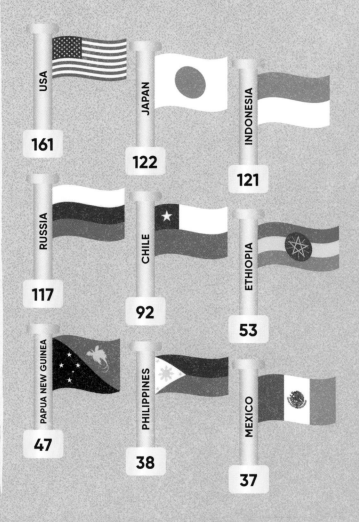

- USA — 161
- JAPAN — 122
- INDONESIA — 121
- RUSSIA — 117
- CHILE — 92
- ETHIOPIA — 53
- PAPUA NEW GUINEA — 47
- PHILIPPINES — 38
- MEXICO — 37

The most earthquake-prone countries

Here are ten countries where you're most likely to feel the earth shake beneath your feet!

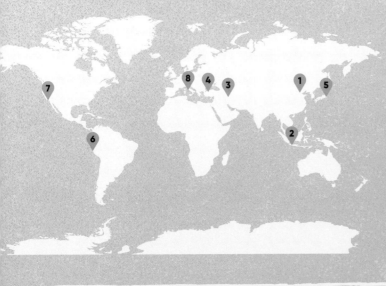

1 China
Since 1900, China has had more than 155 earthquakes of magnitude 7 or above.

2 Indonesia
In 2021 alone, there were four quakes of magnitude 7 or more in Indonesia.

3 Iran
Iran sits at a meeting point of two plates, making it a hotspot for seismic activity.

4 Turkey
Two major fault lines are responsible for the many tremors and quakes here.

5 Japan
The islands of Japan sit where four of the globe's tectonic plates jostle for position.

6 Peru
Sitting between two plates, Peru has had more than 50 big earthquakes since 1900.

7 USA
The West Coast of the US sits on the plates that make up the Ring of Fire.

8 Italy
The southern regions of Italy are where earthquakes are most likely to occur.

Largest earthquakes

Earthquakes are measured on a scale. The ones more than 8 can cause mass destruction, especially if they occur near large cities.

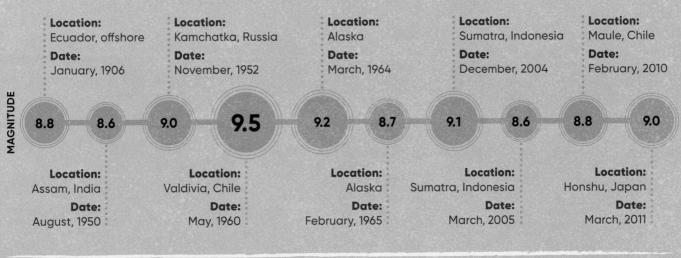

Location: Ecuador, offshore
Date: January, 1906

Location: Kamchatka, Russia
Date: November, 1952

Location: Alaska
Date: March, 1964

Location: Sumatra, Indonesia
Date: December, 2004

Location: Maule, Chile
Date: February, 2010

MAGNITUDE

8.8 · 8.6 · 9.0 · **9.5** · 9.2 · 8.7 · 9.1 · 8.6 · 8.8 · 9.0

Location: Assam, India
Date: August, 1950

Location: Valdivia, Chile
Date: May, 1960

Location: Alaska
Date: February, 1965

Location: Sumatra, Indonesia
Date: March, 2005

Location: Honshu, Japan
Date: March, 2011

Largest tsunamis

Although most tsunamis are small and go by unnoticed, some strong earthquakes can lead to massive tsunamis taller than a skyscraper!

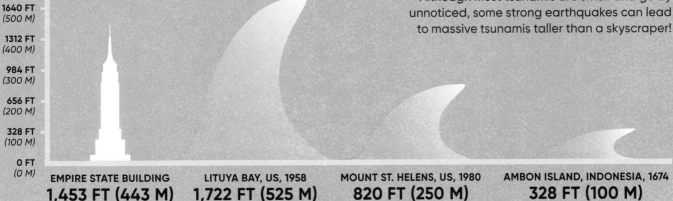

1968 FT (600 M)
1640 FT (500 M)
1312 FT (400 M)
984 FT (300 M)
656 FT (200 M)
328 FT (100 M)
0 FT (0 M)

EMPIRE STATE BUILDING
1,453 FT (443 M)

LITUYA BAY, US, 1958
1,722 FT (525 M)

MOUNT ST. HELENS, US, 1980
820 FT (250 M)

AMBON ISLAND, INDONESIA, 1674
328 FT (100 M)

GLOSSARY

Aa lava
Lava that rips itself apart as it flows, creating a rough and uneven surface.

Active
A volcano that continues to erupt, with magma frequently rising up inside the volcano.

Ash
Tiny bits of magma that explode out of a volcano and cool once in the air.

Atoll
An island made from a ring of coral surrounding a lagoon where a volcanic island once was.

Block lava
Thick and slow lava that cools into chunks of rock.

Body waves
Seismic waves that move under Earth's surface during an earthquake.

Caldera
A wide, deep crater that forms when so much magma erupts from a volcano that it collapses in on itself during an eruption.

Cinder cone
A small, steep volcano that is formed from ash and rock that have spouted out of a volcano.

Crust
Made of solid rock, this is Earth's outer layer. It is the only layer of Earth that people have seen.

Cryovolcano
A volcano found in space that erupts slushy ice instead of magma.

Dormant
A volcano where magma is still present but hasn't erupted for thousands of years.

Earthquake zone
A region that is more likely to experience earthquakes.

Epicenter
The point on Earth's surface directly above the focus of an earthquake.

Extinct
A volcano that cannot erupt again because its magma has completely solidified.

Extrusive
Igneous rock created when magma erupts as lava and then solidifies on Earth's surface.

Fault
A crack in Earth's crust where tectonic plates meet. Earthquakes often occur along these cracks.

Focus
The point where an earthquake begins underground.

Fumarole
A geothermal feature where steam from water boiled deep underground escapes through a crack in Earth's surface.

Geothermal energy
A renewable energy that is created using heat from deep inside Earth.

Geyser
A geothermal feature where hot water from an underground spring occasionally squirts out of the ground.

Guyot
A flat-topped, extinct volcano found underwater.

Hot spring
A geothermal feature where a pond or lake is fed by a constant supply of hot water heated by magma underground.

Hotspot volcano
This volcano forms above a rising bubble of hot mantle rock. The heat from the mantle causes the rock above to melt into magma, which then burns up to the surface to form a volcano.

Hydrothermal vent
A volcanic hot spring that is found on the seabed. It is also known as a black smoker.

Igneous rock
Rock formed when molten rock hardens and becomes solid. Igneous rock can be found above and below Earth's surface.

Igneous intrusion
A rock feature formed by magma cooling within Earth's crust, such as a batholith, sill, or dike.

Inner core
The center of Earth, this layer is made of a molten metal mix of iron, nickel, and other elements.

Intrusive
Igneous rock formed when magma solidifies within Earth's crust.

Landslide
During an earthquake, shakes can disturb rocks, earth, and soil, causing them to slide down the slopes of a mountain or hill.

Lava
Hot, molten rock that erupts from a volcano.

Lava bomb
A blob of lava that cools in the air to form solid rocks.

Lava cave
Once filled with hot, molten lava, these caves are found under the site of an eruption. They are filled with various rock formations.

Liquefaction
A phenomenon where earthquake shakes cause solid soil to liquefy.

Lower mantle
An inner layer of Earth made from very hot, solid rock, which is under great pressure.

Magma
Hot molten rock from Earth's mantle that forms volcanoes where it erupts on the surface.

Magma chamber
A pool of super-hot, molten rock that builds up beneath a volcano.

Magnitude
The number that indicates the strength of an earthquake.

Mercalli Scale
A scale that compares earthquakes according to the amount of damage they do.

Metamorphic rock
Rock formed when older rocks are heated and squeezed deep inside Earth.

Mid-ocean ridge
A mountain range formed in the middle of an ocean, where tectonic plates are pulled apart, causing lava to rise up and harden into rock.

Ocean trench
A deep gulf in the ocean floor, often containing the very deepest parts of the ocean.

Outer core
A dense inner layer of Earth made of liquid metal.

Pahoehoe lava
Thin and runny lava that cools into smooth or wrinkled surfaces.

Pillow lava
Round lumps of rock that form as a result of lava erupting under water.

Pyroclastic flow
A mixture of rock fragments, hot ash, and gas that flows down mountain valleys from an eruption.

Pyroclastic surge
A less dense kind of pyroclastic flow made of a swirling cloud of hot ash and gas that can surge right over ridges.

Rift volcano
A kind of volcano that forms where tectonic plates pull or "rift" apart, allowing hot magma to rise up through the gap.

Ring of Fire
The giant loop of volcanoes lying along the edges of the Pacific Plate. It includes two-thirds of the world's active volcanoes.

Seamount
An underwater volcano that can either be active or inactive.

Sedimentary rock
Rocks formed from squeezed and cemented bits of rock and other materials that settled on the seabed and other places.

Seismic waves
Shockwaves that are created by an earthquake and move both deep inside Earth and on the planet's surface.

Seismogram
A wavy line recording the varying vibrations from an earthquake.

Seismometer
A machine that measures and records the vibrations caused by an earthquake.

Shield volcano
A wide volcano with gently sloping sides, which is formed from many layers of runny lava.

Stratovolcano
A steep-sided volcano built up from hardened layers of lava and ash.

Subduction zone volcano
This volcano forms where one plate is pushed under another. The rock in the sinking plate melts and becomes magma, which then rises through the other plate to form a volcano.

Surface waves
Seismic waves that move on Earth's surface during an earthquake, causing serious damage.

Tectonic plates
The 20 or so gigantic, very slowly shifting slabs of rock that make up Earth's surface.

Tephra
Also known as volcanic fallout, these are solid materials—such as ash and lava bombs—that are thrown out of a volcano during an eruption.

Tsunameter
A machine that picks up pressure changes on the seabed.

Tsunami
A large ocean wave caused by an earthquake on the seabed.

Upper mantle
The top layer of the mantle, directly beneath the crust, extending 416 miles (670 km) down into Earth. It's made of partly melted rock and gets steadily hotter the deeper you go.

Vent
The opening of a volcano, through which an eruption occurs.

Volcanic island
An island formed by a volcano, such as Hawaii, Stromboli, or Surtsey.

Volcanologist
A scientist who studies volcanoes.

ANSWERS

4-5   LAYERED EARTH

BUILD THE PLANET

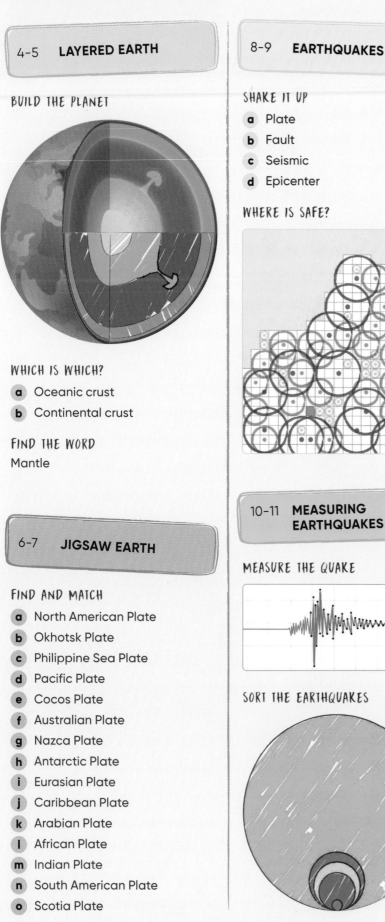

WHICH IS WHICH?
- **a** Oceanic crust
- **b** Continental crust

FIND THE WORD
Mantle

6-7   JIGSAW EARTH

FIND AND MATCH
- **a** North American Plate
- **b** Okhotsk Plate
- **c** Philippine Sea Plate
- **d** Pacific Plate
- **e** Cocos Plate
- **f** Australian Plate
- **g** Nazca Plate
- **h** Antarctic Plate
- **i** Eurasian Plate
- **j** Caribbean Plate
- **k** Arabian Plate
- **l** African Plate
- **m** Indian Plate
- **n** South American Plate
- **o** Scotia Plate

8-9   EARTHQUAKES

SHAKE IT UP
- **a** Plate
- **b** Fault
- **c** Seismic
- **d** Epicenter

WHERE IS SAFE?

10-11   MEASURING EARTHQUAKES

MEASURE THE QUAKE

SORT THE EARTHQUAKES

DRAW THE DAMAGE
Here's what ours look like!

Level 3

Level 5

Level 7

Level 8

12-13   SEISMIC WAVES

FINISH THE PICTURE

TRUE OR FALSE?
- **a** False (S waves can only travel through solid rock.)
- **b** True
- **c** True
- **d** False (P waves are the fastest type of seismic wave.)

14-15   BUILDING FOR EARTHQUAKES

MATCH THE SAFETY SYSTEMS
- **a** Taipei 101, Taiwan
- **b** Philippine Arena, Philippines
- **c** Burj Khalifa, UAE
- **d** Transamerica Pyramid, US

FIND THE CITY
Tokyo

BE AN ARCHITECT
Here's what ours looks like!

16-17 SHAKING UP THE LANDSCAPE

DRAW THE HOUSES
Here's what ours look like!

Sandy soil   Clay / Silt soil

CHANGE THE SCENE

1 Before the landslide

2 Landslide underway

3 The lake is gone

FILL THE GAPS
Rockfall

18-19 TSUNAMIS

DETECT A TSUNAMI
a Satellite
b Surface buoy
c Tsunameter

TAKE A TSUNAMI QUIZ
a An earthquake
b Harbor wave
c It rises up.
d It signals to a buoy.

BONUS QUESTION
500 mph (800 kmph)

WHICH IS WHICH?
a Undersea quake
b Making waves
c Danger!

20-21 EARTHQUAKE QUIZ

1 a. Seismic
2 True
3 a. Fault
4 True
5 d. Railway lines badly damaged
6 P waves
7 a. Taipei 101, Taiwan
   b. Transamerica Pyramid, US
8 True
9 b. Significant
10 c. Liquefaction
11 True
12 a. Inner core
   b. Lower mantle
13 False (it's when rocks fall downhill)
14 True
15 d. Chile
16 Focus
17 True

22-23 HOW VOLCANOES FORM

WHICH IS WHICH?
a Subduction zone
b Rift
c Hotspot

FIND THE WORD
1 Basalt
2 Mountain

FINISH THE PICTURE

BONUS QUESTION
Stratovolcano

24-25 INSIDE A VOLCANO

WHICH IS WHICH?
a Lava flow
b Magma chamber
c Secondary vent
d Volcanic ash
e Secondary conduit

BUILD THE VOLCANO

LABEL IT
a Volcanic ash
b Main vent
c Main conduit
d Layers of lava and ash
e Magma chamber

26-27 WHICH VOLCANO?

WHICH IS WHICH?
Whakaari, Stratovolcano
Mountain of Lagi, Cinder cone
Erta Ale, Shield volcano
Karymsky, Stratovolcano
Santa Ana Volcano, Caldera
Skjaldbreiður, Shield volcano

MAKE A VOLCANIC CHART

a
Cinder cone

b
Stratovolcano

c
Caldera

d
Shield volcano

DRAW CINDER CONES
Here's what ours look like!

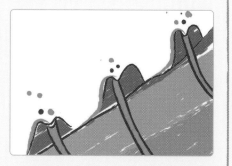

28-29 THE RING OF FIRE

LEARN THE FACTS
Mount Fuji
Location: Japan
Height: 12,388 ft (3,776 m)

Mount St Helens
Type: Stratovolcano
Last major eruption: 1980

Nevado Del Ruiz
Location: Colombia

LOCATE THE VOLCANOES

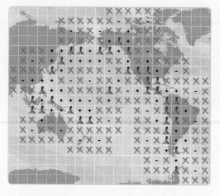

30-31 LAVA!

FILL IN THE FLOW CHART
a Does it form underwater?
b Is the surface rough
and uneven?
c Pahoehoe lava
d Block lava

WHICH IS WHICH?
a Runny river
b Lava lake
c Explosion
d Into the sea
e Slow and steady

FIND THE LAVA
Pillow lava

32-33 VOLCANIC ROCKS

FILL THE ROCK

COMPLETE THE ROCK-DOKU

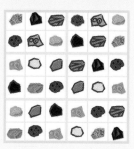

BONUS QUESTION
Marble, Limestone

MATCH IT
a Limestone
b Pumice
c Obsidian
d Marble
e Granite
f Basalt

34-35 LAVA CAVES

MATCH THE STAGES
a 2
b 1
c 5
d 4
e 3

COMPLETE THE FEATURES
Here's what ours look like!

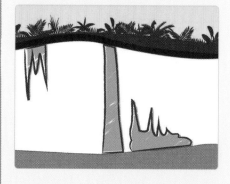

36-37 ERUPTIONS

FIND THE PATH

LOCATE THE ERUPTION

CAN YOU FEEL THE PRESSURE?

- **a** 9
- **b** 17, this is likely to erupt first
- **c** 15

38-39 TYPES OF ERUPTION

WHICH IS WHICH?

- **a** Strombolian
- **b** Icelandic
- **c** Plinian
- **d** Pelean
- **e** Vulcanian
- **f** Hawaiian

DRAW THE ERUPTIONS

a | **b**

Hawaiian | Plinian

c | **d**

Pelean | Icelandic

e | **f**

Vulcanian | Strombolian

40-41 PYROCLASTIC ERUPTIONS

WHICH IS WHICH?

- **a** Flow
- **b** Surge

COLOR IN THE ISLAND

FIND THE VOLCANO
Pelée

42-43 VOLCANIC FALLOUT

HOW FAR WILL I GO?

0.6 mile (1 km)
Lava bombs

15.5 miles (25 km)
Lapilli

**620 miles+
(1,000 km+)**
Volcanic ash

TRACK THE ERUPTION

CRACK THE CODE
Tephra

NAME THE FALLOUT

- **a** Lapilli
- **b** Lava bomb
- **c** Volcanic ash

44-45 KRAKATAU

DRAW THE BLAST

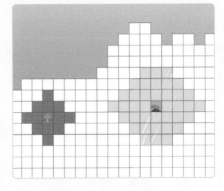

RE-CREATE THE ISLAND

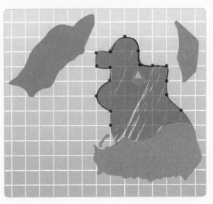

MATCH THE MAPS

- **a** 1883
- **b** 1880
- **c** 1927

46-47 IT'S GONNA BLOW!

DRAW THE TOOLS

CHOOSE THE ALERT LEVEL

▲ **Kilauea**
Alert Level: Warning

▲ **Karymsky**
Alert Level: Watch

▲ **Parinacota**
Alert Level: Normal

48-49 ROBOTS

WHICH ROBOT?

a TrackWalker II

b VolcanoBot 1

c Research drone

d Dante II

NAME THE VOLCANOES

a Mount Bromo, Indonesia

b Mount Semeru, Indonesia

c Mount Fagradalsfjall, Iceland

d Mount Nyiragongo, Democratic
Republic of the Congo

DESIGN YOUR OWN ROBOT

Here's what ours looks like!

50-51 IS IT ACTIVE?

COLOR IN THE VOLCANOES

ACTIVE, DORMANT, OR EXTINCT?

WILL IT ERUPT?

Mount Kilimanjaro
Dormant

Mount Fuji
Active

Ben Nevis
Extinct

52-53 VOLCANOES AND THE CLIMATE

COLOR THE ASH CLOUD

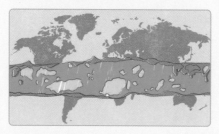

LIGHT UP THE CLOUDS

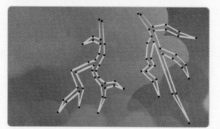

GET THROUGH THE ASH

54-55 AFTER THE ERUPTION

FIND THE NUTRIENTS

COMPLETE THE TIMELINE

a 20 years later

b 10 years later

c 1 year later

d Day 1

WHERE TO FARM?

FINISH THE MOSAIC

WHICH IS WHICH?

a Loaf of bread
b Dog
c Mosaic
d Glass jar
e Bronze Medusa

WHAT HAPPENED?

Here's what ours look like!

12pm   2pm

5pm   5:30pm

11:15pm   12am

FIND THE DIAMONDS

NUMBER OF DIAMONDS
5

WHO'S WHO?

a Kemi
b Violet
c Alex

LABEL THE PLANT

a Steam
b Generator
c Pump
d Water
e Hot rocks

FIND THE PATH

CHOOSE THE BEST NEST
c Cozy hot sand on top of crater

FIND THE WORD
Extremophiles

GUESS WHO?
Flamingo

MATCH THE FACTS

a Mount Erebus
b Mount Melbourne
c Mount Erebus
d Mount Terror

FIND MOUNT EREBUS
J,3

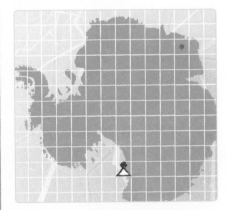

NAME THE VOLCANO
Erebus

WHICH VOLCANO IS WHERE?

a Venus
b Mars
c Jupiter
d Mercury
e Saturn
f Neptune

HOW BIG IS THE VOLCANO?

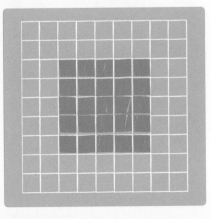

66-67 VOLCANIC LANDFORMS

FIND THE FORMATIONS

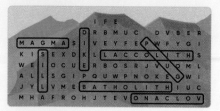

NAME THAT FEATURE

Sugar Loaf Mountain, Brazil
What am I? Exposed batholith

Pilanesberg, South Africa
What am I? Ring dike

Ship Rock, USA
What am I? Volcanic plug

EXTRUSIVE OR INTRUSIVE?

a Extrusive
b Intrusive

HOW DID IT LOOK?

Here's what ours looks like!

68-69 HOT SPRINGS AND GEYSERS

SKETCH THE SCENE

FIGURE OUT THE FEATURE

a Mudpot
b Geyser
c Hot spring
d Fumarole

COLOR THE HOT SPRING

70-71 YELLOWSTONE

COLOR THE ASH

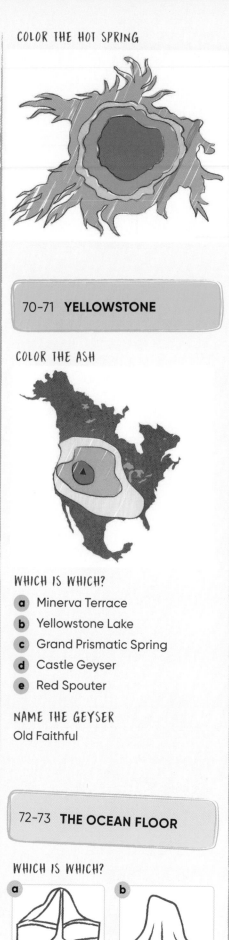

WHICH IS WHICH?

a Minerva Terrace
b Yellowstone Lake
c Grand Prismatic Spring
d Castle Geyser
e Red Spouter

NAME THE GEYSER

Old Faithful

72-73 THE OCEAN FLOOR

WHICH IS WHICH?

a

b

Volcanic island   Guyot

Mid-ocean ridge

Ocean trench

Seamount

TRENCH OR RIDGE?

a Ridge
b Trench

FIND THE FEATURES

a Guyot
b Mid-ocean ridge
c Ocean trench
d Seamount
e Volcanic island

74-75 DEEP-SEA VENTS

BUILD A VENT

Here's what ours looks like!

MATCH THE DEEP DIVERS

a AUTOSUB600
b Alvin
c HROV Nereus

SEARCH BELOW

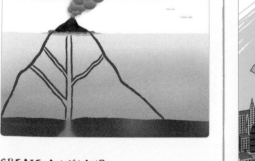

FIND THE ANIMALS

Light shrimp

Yeti crab

Pale octopus

76-77 VOLCANIC ISLANDS

FINISH THE PICTURE

CREATE AN ISLAND

Spiders

Seeds

Tufts of grass

Birds

WHICH IS WHICH?

a Active volcano

b Sinking island

c Atoll and lagoon

78-79 UNIQUE VOLCANOES

QUIZ YOURSELF

a Mount Nyiragongo

b Sulfur

c Cone

d 1774

WHERE IN THE WORLD?

80-81 VOLCANO QUIZ

1 d. VolcanoBot 1
2 False (it is hundreds of volcanoes located around the Pacific Ocean)
3 b. Stratovolcano, Japan
4 c. Krakatau
5 Diamond
6 b. Yeti crabs
7 a. Pumice, c. Basalt
8 c. Hotspot
9 True (it is Olympus Mons)
10 c. Eeek
11 Dormant
12 Volcanologist
13 Pyroclastic surge
14 b. Mount Vesuvius
15 Extinct
16 b. Fly Ranch Geyser

82-83 VOLCANO!

DRAW YOUR OWN!
Here's what ours looks like!

INDEX

ACKNOWLEDGMENTS

DK would like to thank the following for their help with this book:
Catharine Robertson for proofreading; Elizabeth Wise for compiling the
index; Rebecca Fry, Rona Skene, Ian Fitzgerald, Andrea Page, and Elizabeth
Blakemore for editorial assistance; Gilda Pacitti for design assistance;
Phil Gamble, Mark Clifton, and Gus Scott for additional illustrations;
Laura Gardner for additional jacket design.

DK would like to thank the following for their
kind permission to reproduce their photographs:

(Key: a-above; b-below/bottom; c-center; f-far; l-left; r-right; t-top)

18 Shutterstock.com: Lyu Hu (tr). **20 Dreamstime.com:** Chih Chang Chou (bc);
Frank Fell (br). **22 Dreamstime.com:** Frank Bach (cl); Bennymarty (bl). **Getty
Images:** guenterguni (clb). **26 Alamy Stock Photo:** Maurice Brand (bc).
Dreamstime.com: Elena Gurdina (cr); Jjfarq (cra). **Getty Images / iStock:** thopson
(ca). **Shutterstock.com:** maramade (c); Wirestock Creators (br). **27 Alamy Stock
Photo:** Melinda Podor (bl). **28 Alamy Stock Photo:** Mauricio Alvadorado /
COLPRENSA / Xinhua (br). **Dreamstime.com:** Hiro1775 (clb); Tusharkoley (cb).
30 Alamy Stock Photo: Paolo Patrizi (cra/Block); Doug Perrine (cra). **Dreamstime.
com:** Vulkanette (cr). **Shutterstock.com:** Shane Myers Photography (tr). **31 Alamy
Stock Photo:** Roger Coulam (ca/a). **Getty Images / iStock:** mlharing (cla).
Shutterstock.com: Yvonne Baur (c); Michail_Vorobyev (ca/b); beboy (cra). **33
Dorling Kindersley:** Colin Keates / Natural History Museum, London (cb); Gary
Ombler, Oxford University Museum of Natural History (c); Harry Taylor / Trustees
of the National Museums Of Scotland (clb). **40 Alamy Stock Photo:** REUTERS /
Dwi Oblo (tr). **43 Alamy Stock Photo:** RGB Ventures / SuperStock (bc); Richard

Roscoe / Stocktrek Images (br). **Shutterstock.com:** Tanguy de Saint-Cyr (bc/a).
47 Dreamstime.com: Kseniya Ragozina (br). **Getty Images:** Jim Sugar (bl).
Shutterstock.com: Atly (bc). **49 Shutterstock.com:** Rainer Albiez (tc/b); Sugrit
Jiranarak (tl); ImageBank4u (tc); Christopher Horsley (tr). **51 Dreamstime.com:**
Sean Pavone / Sepavo (c). **Shutterstock.com:** John A Cameron (cr). **52 Alamy
Stock Photo:** imageBROKER / Cornelius Paas (br). **Shutterstock.com:**
Photovolcanica.com (tr). **53 Alamy Stock Photo:** Xinhua / Rouelle Umali (cla).
55 Alamy Stock Photo: David Hayes (ca/Ferns); PRILL Mediendesign (cla).
Dreamstime.com: Industryandtravel (ca). **Getty Images:** Jim Sugar (br). **56
Getty Images / iStock:** boerescul (cl). **57 Alamy Stock Photo:** Artokoloro (cla);
Azoor Photo (cra/d); Stefano Ravera (cra). **Dorling Kindersley:** James Stevenson
/ Museo Archeologico Nazionale di Napoli (cla/a). **Dreamstime.com:** Gianni
Marchetti (ca). **61 Alamy Stock Photo:** Oleksandr Tkachenko (bl). **Science Photo
Library:** Eye Of Science (cr). **62 Alamy Stock Photo:** Xinhua / Zhu Jichai (crb).
Shutterstock.com: Michael Lodge (clb); bruno pagnanelli (cb). **63 Shutterstock.
com:** Applejak (br). **64 NASA:** JHUAPL / SWRI (tr). **67 NASA:** Jesse Allen / Adam
Voiland (c). **Shutterstock.com:** Sean Pavone (cr); Arkadij Schell (cla) **68 Alamy
Stock Photo:** Prisma by Dukas Presseagentur GmbH (tr). **71 Alamy Stock Photo:**
Stephen Coyne (cr). **Dreamstime.com:** Kenneth Sponsler (tr). **Getty Images /
iStock:** barbaraaaa (c); swisshippo (tc); Ajith Kumar (cra). **73 Getty Images /
iStock:** ratpack223 (tr). **77 Alamy Stock Photo:** FLPA (tl). **78 Shutterstock.com:**
Ashim D Silva (cr); StanislavBeloglazov (c). **79 Dreamstime.com:** Puripat
Lertpunyaroj (c). **Shutterstock.com:** Mazur Travel (cl). **80 Dorling Kindersley:** Colin
Keates / Natural History Museum, London (br). **Shutterstock.com:** Christopher
Horsley (c). **81 Shutterstock.com:** Photovolcanica.com (crb); WR Studios (cra)

All other images © Dorling Kindersley